Following the surrender of France in Jun   self
against a potential German invasion. In gr   ...was taken to establish an elite bodyguard to protect the British Royal Family. Led initially by Major
Jimmy Coats, a Coldstream Guards officer and celebrated winter sportsman, it
was given the innocuous title of 'The Coats Mission', but its proposed role was
perhaps the most important assigned to any unit in the British armed forces. It
was intended that this group would evacuate King George VI, Queen Elizabeth
and the two princesses, Margaret and her sister Elizabeth, to a place of safety
away from London.

For the next two years it trained and prepared for the role in the face of what
was believed to be a very real threat, and this study, drawing on previously unseen
documents, interviews and archival material, provides its history and explains
how the Royal Family's protection was viewed. Beginning with the pre-war
shelter preparations for the Royal Households and running through the increased
anxiety of the 1940 invasion threat and Blitz, the renewed danger in 1941 and
then the progressive reduction in the special measures in the years that followed,
The King's Private Army offers the first dedicated account of a largely unknown
but potentially critical element of the defence of the United Kingdom during the
Second World War.

Dr Andrew Stewart is a Reader in Conflict and Diplomacy in the Defence Studies Department, King's College London. In addition to a large number of journal articles and edited volumes, he is the author of several books about the Second World War including most recently *Caen Controversy: The Battle for Sword Beach 1944* (published by Helion & Company in 2014).

THE KING'S PRIVATE ARMY

PROTECTING THE BRITISH ROYAL FAMILY DURING THE SECOND WORLD WAR

Andrew Stewart

Helion & Company

Helion & Company Limited
26 Willow Road
Solihull
West Midlands
B91 1UE
England
Tel. 0121 705 3393
Fax 0121 711 4075
Email: info@helion.co.uk
Website: www.helion.co.uk
Twitter: @helionbooks
Visit our blog http://blog.helion.co.uk/

Published by Helion & Company 2015
Designed and typeset by Mach 3 Solutions Ltd, Bussage, Gloucestershire
Cover designed by Paul Hewitt, Battlefield Design (www.battlefield-design.co.uk)
Printed by Henry Ling Limited, Dorchester, Dorset

ISBN 978-1-910777-28-2

British Library Cataloguing-in-Publication Data.
A catalogue record for this book is available from the British Library.

For details of other military history titles published by Helion & Company Limited
contact the above address, or visit our website: http://www.helion.co.uk.

We always welcome receiving book proposals from prospective authors.

Contents

List of Illustrations & Maps

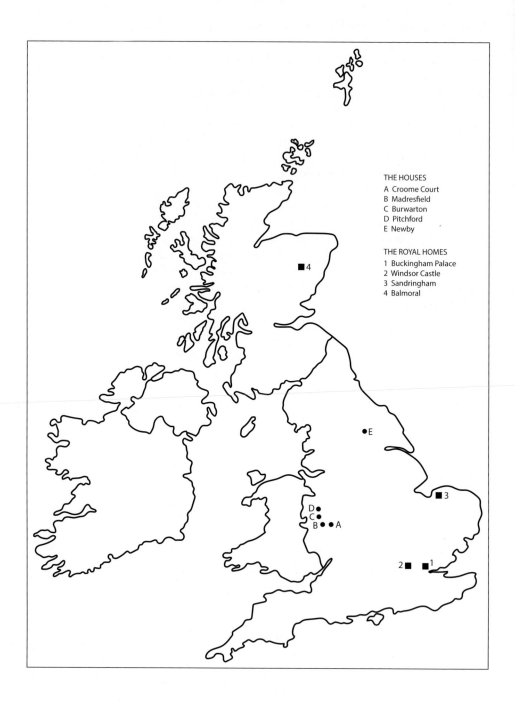

THE HOUSES
A Croome Court
B Madresfield
C Burwarton
D Pitchford
E Newby

THE ROYAL HOMES
1 Buckingham Palace
2 Windsor Castle
3 Sandringham
4 Balmoral

Introduction

The security of Britain's Royal Family during the Second World War has not previously been examined in any detail. In large part this is a reflection of the success that was achieved in gathering and destroying any information that related to the detailed plans that were developed from the summer of 1940 onwards when the country faced up to the possibility of an invasion. As with the post-war secrecy that was attached to the successful penetration of German signals intelligence, more commonly referred to as 'Ultra', official efforts were made to prevent the preparations that had been made from becoming common knowledge. There was not, however, any similar effort to absolutely prevent those involved from discussing this aspect of their wartime experiences and two brief accounts were published. These took the form of regimental histories or were published in military journals which had only very limited circulations. At the same time, the number of those who had been involved was relatively small and the process involved with their initial selection ensured that their discretion could be assured; post-war this meant there was a natural reluctance to discuss the role they had played. Added to this, of course, was the reality that nothing actually happened in so much as there was no invasion and no need for the plans that had been prepared to be put into action. A very strong narrative therefore developed in the years following the end of the war which sought generally to limit any discussion about what might have happened to King George VI, his wife Queen Elizabeth and their two daughters, Elizabeth and Margaret Rose, in the event of Britain appearing to be on the point of defeat. As a result the now commonly accepted idea is that there were no detailed plans for the Royal Family's wartime protection which involved the potential for them being evacuated.

Post-war this position has held true and as a result there continues even now to be very little discussion of the subject.[1] This stems in large part from some of the earliest brief references such as that produced by the celebrated writer and war hero Peter Fleming. He had been centrally involved in secret activities throughout the war first as a leading member of the Auxiliaries, an irregular militia established to harry any German forces occupying a conquered Britain, and then as part of the Special Operations Executive which carried out attacks against enemies

---

1   In September 2015 Her Majesty Queen Elizabeth II became the longest-reigning sovereign surpassing Queen Victoria. This led to considerable media coverage about her life but even within this there was barely any reference to the wartime years. Typical was Robert Jobson, writing in the London *Evening Standard*, who claimed that "talk of [the princesses] leaving the country for their own safety was quickly dismissed"; Robert Jobson, 'Love, war and loss: How Lilibet grew up to become Queen', *Evening Standard*, Monday 7 September 2015, pp.8-9

overseas. In researching the possibility of a German invasion during the war years he had corresponded with Queen Elizabeth, by this stage referred to as the Queen Mother following her husband's death in 1952, and identified that steps had been taken to make some preparations.[2] Nonetheless he concluded that there was never really any idea of the Royal Family leaving the country and "if any proposals of this nature had been made to the King they would have been received very ill and rejected out of hand". This was because there was an "instinctive inhibition" in regard to "the consideration, let alone the adoption, of any measures which might have implied a lack of faith in the nation's power to defend itself". The idea that the sovereign might have left Britain was not a possibility, even the "minor and uncontroversial alternative", the possibility of sending the two princesses overseas was simply not considered and he concluded that no decision or communiqué was ever issued. Much the same conclusion was made the same year by the King's official biographer who also made only very limited reference to plans in the event of an invasion. He refers to "speedy evacuation … from London" but also utterly refuted the idea that either King or Queen would leave the country.[3]

Despite the passage of time the Queen Mother's official biographer, in a much more recent volume more than 1000 pages in length, can also only find five sentences on the matter and provides even less detail than the earlier volume.[4] The most recent account of the Royal Family during the war years devotes even less consideration, a single sentence referring to "the feeling of security" that was "finally established with armoured cars on standby at the palace and an escort selected from the Brigade of Guards and the Household Cavalry".[5] Each of these authors had full access to the Royal Archives and yet they could either not find any more specific information or, which is much more likely, chose not to make more detailed reference to the documents that are known to exist.[6] Such omissions highlight the sense that there has been considerable secrecy attached to the plans, both during and after the war, for reasons which are not entirely clear and which detract from the popular understanding of the wartime years. As this study will show a personal bodyguard was in fact created, for which there were no written orders other than in the event of an emergency it was to escort the

2   Peter Fleming to Sir Michael (?), 27 September 1955, Peter Fleming Papers, University of Reading Museums and Special Collections Service, MS 1391, A7 (hereafter 'UoR); Peter Fleming, *Invasion 1940* (London; Hart Davis, 1957), pp.132-133

3   John W. Wheeler-Bennett, *King George VI – His Life and Reign* (London; Macmillan and Co. Ltd., 1958), pp.463-464

4   William Shawcross, *Queen Elizabeth the Queen Mother: The Official Biography* (London; Pan, 2010), p.517

5   Deborah Cadbury, *Princes at War: The British Royal Family's Private Battle in the Second World War* (London; Bloomsbury, 2015), p.166

6   Despite an extended correspondence with the Royal Archives about this project no access was granted to the relevant files with "security implications" being cited as the reason why this would not be possible; Stewart to Royal Archives, 12 May 2010; Stewart to Royal Archives, 8 July 2010; Miss Pamela Clark (Royal Archives) to Stewart, 11 October 2010; Clark to Stewart, 14 December 2010; Stewart to Royal Archives, 15 June 2015; Clark to Stewart, 9 July 2015 (email)

King, Queen and their children to a place of safety and protect them by all means available. The official version has, however, consistently refused to acknowledge that this entirely prudent and reasonable defensive measure was taken. Indeed the possibility of moving the monarch in the event of invasion was nothing new. If Napoleon had landed on Britain's southern coast in 1805 preparations had been made for King George III to have been moved from Windsor further inland to Worcestershire and away from any advancing French forces.[7] As another European dictator once again threatened the continent's peace and security a plan was in fact developed which appeared remarkably similar to its only known predecessor in so much as it sought to move the monarch and his family away from the likely front-lines. Its success was of the utmost importance, their capture carried with it the potential to deliver a devastating blow to any attempts to resist an attack against the British Isles.

Despite the challenges that have presented themselves it has nonetheless been possible to piece together an account of how the Royal Family were to have been protected if the Germans had attempted an invasion. In large part this has been made possible by the many individuals who have been willing to offer advice or information and I would like to extend my sincere thanks to the following: Michael Anson; Pat (and Richard) Beighton; Hugh Boscawen; Jeff Carpenter; Rhys Cazenove; Major Robert Cazenove (RHQ Coldstream Guards); Mike Galer (Senior Keeper of Military and Social History, Derby Museums and Art Gallery); Stuart Gill; Charlie Hancock; Richard Hancock; Emma Hancox (Historic Environment and Archaeology Service, Worcestershire); Patricia Harling; P. Hatfield (College Archivist, Eton); Peter Hughes (Madresfield Court); John Lloyd (Museum Manager, Household Cavalry Museum Archive); Derek Notley (Coldstream Guards Association); Lieutenant Colonel (Retd.) Sir Julian Paget; Neil Paterson (Metropolitan Police Heritage Centre); Tony Perfect; Crispin Powell (Archivist, Northamptonshire Record Office); C/Sgt (Retd.) Jeffrey Robinson (Coldstream Guards Association); Paul Robinson (Curator, Northamptonshire Regiment and Northamptonshire Yeomanry Collections); Colonel Rob Sergeant (Coldstream Guards); Mary-Anne Sergison-Brooke; Lieutenant Colonel C.J.E. Seymour (Regimental Archivist, Grenadier Guards); Geoff Sherwood; Steve Snelling; Brigadier (Retd.) Peter Stewart-Richardson; Jill Tovey (Croome Court); Colonel (Retd.) K.M. Tutt OBE (Adjutant General's Corps Museum Collection); Colonel (Retd.) Simon Vandeleur (Regimental Adjutant, RHQ Coldstream Guards); Mick Wilks; David Winpenny.

Special mention must be made of Brigadier (Retd.) Sir Jeffrey Darell, Bt., M.C. who, before his death in 2013, kindly shared his recollections of the period he

---

7   According to one local historian this was Hartlebury Castle, the long-standing home of Bishops of Worcester; Jeff Carpenter, *Wartime Worcestershire* (Studley; Brewin Books, 1995), p.22

spent serving in the Coats Mission. Added to this the printed matter he also shared had made a significant contribution to the writing of this book.

In addition I would like to thank the staff of the following archives and libraries for their assistance whilst I was undertaking research for the project: the National Archives, London; the Imperial War Museum, London; the Liddell Hart Centre for Military Archives, King's College London; the National Army Museum, London; and finally both the King's College London Library and the Joint Services Command and Staff College Library. Where relevant and appropriate I must thank the trustees or similar of those archives above that have kindly granted access and for permission for the use of selected brief quotations. The material examined has proven to be of considerable benefit to the study.

I am most grateful to Andrea Jackson and Luke Vivian-Neal who completed research for me in the National Archives.

The encouragement and support provided by Duncan Rogers, Managing Director of Helion and Company Limited, throughout the production of this book has been most welcome. His growing success is a reflection of the most positive attitude he displays towards military history writing. I very much look forward to working with him over the coming years.

I am extremely fortunate to enjoy the continuing encouragement of my parents who have helped me throughout my career. My wife Joanne makes considerable sacrifices in terms of the time we are able to spend together and I can only thank her for her support without which it would not be possible to undertake these projects. As with all of my projects there have been many friends and acquaintances that have offered assistance when required and I am also grateful to them. This particular book is dedicated to David Steeds who has been a great mentor since my undergraduate days; I am indebted to him for the advice and guidance he has offered over nearly 25 years which has helped make me a better scholar and writer than would otherwise have been the case.

The analysis, opinions and conclusions expressed or implied are those of the author and do not represent the views of the Joint Services Command and Staff College, the Royal College of Defence Studies, the UK Ministry of Defence or any other government agency. Any errors of fact are the responsibility of the author and, if notified, every reasonable effort will be made to correct them.

Oxford, September 2015

1

Preparing for War

It is far from correct to believe that preparations for war only began with any real seriousness following the Munich crisis in September 1938 and the ensuing realisation that the German leader, Adolf Hitler, could not be appeased with a diplomatic solution to his territorial ambitions.[1] The Defence Requirements Committee met for the first time in November 1933 and quickly reached the conclusion that Britain's "ultimate potential enemy" was Germany and from this point on steps began to be taken to provide regular updates in the government's War Book.[2] With inputs from each Whitehall department and agency this guide detailed the steps that would need to be taken in the event of war to allow the country to continue functioning. As part of this process, and the same month as the Air Raid Precautions Act was passed by Parliament in December 1937, a sub-committee chaired by Sir James Rae, a senior official in the Treasury, produced a highly secret report which contained information about how the evacuation of Whitehall departments would be conducted.[3] This expanded upon the earlier work that had been undertaken by Warren Fisher whose committee's report the previous winter offered a basis for the later study.[4] Essentially the British government was faced with the choice between evacuation, dispersal and secrecy and fortification. So sensitive were Rae's plans, which pointed to the first of these, that in his obituary, published following his death twenty years later, no reference was made to the role he had played or even to the committee's existence.[5] This was not because he had enjoyed a career complete with more interesting events and details to record. Rae had clearly been a most competent civil servant and had sat on numerous panels and committees. In terms of impact on the country's security none of his other roles compared with the time he had spent considering how Britain would continue to operate in the event of devastating air attacks destroying its capital in the first days of any potential future conflict.

The omission also avoided highlighting the single still redacted word in this report, referred to as '50', which was the location for where the Royal Family

---

1 Basil Collier, *The Defence of the United Kingdom (History of the Second World War)* (London; Her Majesty's Stationary Office, 1957), pp.1-75
2 Ibid., p.25
3 Committee of Imperial Defence, 'Sub-Committee to Prepare Plans for the Location and Accommodation of Staffs of Government Departments in Time of War', D.S.(P) Series, 30 November 1937, CAB16/155, The National Archives, Kew (hereafter 'TNA')
4 Deputy Chiefs of Staff Memorandum (18), 17 November 1936, CAB54/3, TNA
5 'Obituary – Sir James Rae', *The Times*, 4 November 1957

were to be evacuated.[6] With security considerations dictating that just one full copy of the Rae document was ever produced, the remainder used code-names which required an apparently long-lost cipher to identify the various locations. In mid-January 1938 the King's private secretary was shown the unedited version and briefed on the details along with the proposed plan to evacuate the House of Parliament, House of Lords and the government.[7] The Rae Committee had proposed a two-stage move away from London if it were under attack.[8] The first of these, referred to as the 'Yellow Move', would involve some 44,000 staff moving out of the capital to the provinces where they would begin the transfer of the running of their respective departments and agencies. The second, to be undertaken once the anticipated destruction of any assault on London had made continuing governmental work impossible, the 'Black Move', would see the move of a further 16,000 key personnel from the remaining ministries, along with the prime minister and his cabinet, the members of both the House of Commons and House of Lords, and now also the Royal Family. In briefing King George VI, who was staying at Sandringham, Sir Alexander Hardinge gave him the details of the preparations that had been made at the selected location where the Office of Works had already undertaken some work to provide suitable air raid precautions.[9]

While the exact location is not known, the remainder of the text in the document does make it clear that the property was to be near the sites chosen for the government's key officials, and in order to keep the King fully informed as to the state of the war it had to allow Privy Councillors and, presumably, his prime minister to attend as required. In their search for potential locations for 'nerve centres' where the state's key bodies and individuals could be moved in any future emergency, civil servants surveyed the whole of the country but particular focus was attached to the West Country looking for suitable buildings to be used for office-space and accommodation. In January 1939 the GPO advised that the area of Evesham, Cheltenham, Gloucester, Hereford and Worcester would be preferable in terms of being able to provide the most effective communications.[10] A number of sites were identified including Stratford-upon-Avon to which the House of Commons and the House of Lords were to head to use the theatre as a venue for their meetings. Key figures of state would be dispersed in various

---

6   'Sub-Committee to Prepare Plans for the Location…', 30 November 1937, CAB16/155, TNA. Warren Fisher's committee had merely agreed that it would be necessary to determine if the King and the Royal Family intended to remain in London or not

7   Sir Maurice Hankey to Sir Alexander Hardinge, 5 January 1938, CAB21/2637, TNA

8   Mick Wilks, *The Defence of Worcestershire and the Southern Approaches to Birmingham in World War II* (Little Logaston; Logaston Press, 2007), pp.22-23

9   Hardinge to Hankey, 7 January 1938, CAB21/2637, TNA; ibid., 'Sub-Committee to Prepare Plans for the Location…', 30 November 1937, CAB16/155

10 Note by de Normann, 20 January 1939, WORK28/21, TNA. The largely rural county of Worcestershire, in the heart of Britain and at the furthest point from the coast, was almost inevitably attractive to those in London who had been tasked with planning.

country houses in the vicinity. Hindlip Hall, north of Worcester was identified as the temporary home for the Cabinet and Spetchley Manor nearby was to be used by the prime minister and his staff. In terms of finding a suitable location for the Royal Family, Croome Court near Severn Stoke in Worcestershire certainly fulfilled the criteria adopted by the Office of Works. A large country house set in a surrounding 15,000 acre estate it was the ancestral home of the Earl of Coventry and known to the King and Queen who had stayed there during the pre-war period.[11] Hindlip was only 12 miles away and it was just eight miles to Spetchley making it ideally situated as a potential refuge.

Whilst the Royal Archives can find no reference connecting the Royal Family to the house during the Second World War, one historian's research points to Croome having been identified to take on this hugely important role.[12] With the Assistant Master of the Household, Ririd Myddleton, taking the lead in discussions accommodation arrangements were reportedly confirmed in the final days of August 1939; this argument is supported by information held in archives connected to Croome which also point to plans being drawn up at this stage for allotting rooms to the potential Royal party.[13] Five weeks later Sir Patrick Duff, a senior official in the Office of Works who had been responsible for organising many of the most sensitive details relating to the evacuation plans, confirmed that a refuge was being constructed at this site.[14] Although the identity of the refuge initially selected for the Royal Family therefore remains officially unknown it would not be unreasonable to say that it was Croome Court which by the war's outbreak had most likely assumed the role.

As for its potential future guests the Royal Family had spent the weeks immediately prior to the declaration of war at Balmoral. Like so many other key figures within the British establishment, even at this late stage the King and Queen believed that there would be no war and that "Hitler's bluff would be called".[15] As the situation worsened the King returned to London on 23 August with his wife following him five days later. With the declaration of war the Cabinet ordered preliminary measures for a complete evacuation of all government staff but went no further for fear of the effects on public morale.[16] The two Princesses, however,

11 Hilda Newman (with Tim Tate), *Diamonds at Dinner: My Life as a Lady's Maid in a 1930s Stately Home* (London; John Blake Publishing Ltd., 2013), pp.25-42, 64-67
12 Pamela Clark cited in correspondence with Tim Hickson (Friends of Croome Court), 11 January 2011; Howarth to Bridges, 12 September 1939, CAB21/608, TNA; Research by Richard Beighton, n.d. (2002?), Although the researcher passed away in July 2011 some of his notes were found in Brigadier Jeffrey Darell's correspondence
13 'The role of Croome Court during WW2 – Evidence from the Croome Archive', supplied by Jill Tovey (Archivist to Croome Court), January 2011; Sarah Kay, 'Croome Redefined – Conservation Management and Maintenance Place', National Trust, 6 June 2012, p.133
14 Research by Richard Beighton
15 Sir Miles Lampson Diary, 29 August 1939, cited in Sarah Bradford, *Elizabeth – A Biography of Her Majesty The Queen* (London; Heinemann, 1996), p.87
16 War Cabinet Meeting (39)6, 6 September 1939, CAB65/1/6, TNA

were sent to the Aberdeenshire estate of Birkhall, their parents' longstanding favourite summer home, under the care of an equerry, their nanny Clara 'Alah' Knight and 'holiday governess' Georgina Guérin, and a chauffeur. There was also a police sergeant, a Sergeant Gordon, and two constables all from the special 'Travelling Staff' protection detail based at Canon Row.[17] Later they were joined by their Scottish governess, Marion Crawford, at which point their schooling resumed.[18] In addition to the lessons at Birkhall Elizabeth studied constitutional history as a correspondence course with Henry Marten, the Vice-Provost of Eton, setting and marking the papers, and a French teacher, Mrs Montaudon-Smith, joined the staff.[19] Having not seen their father for four months they travelled to Sandringham just before Christmas to join their parents and – despite the possible German threat – spent six weeks with them.[20] From there they did not travel back to Scotland but, during the first week of February 1940, they were moved to the Royal Lodge which was three miles from Windsor Castle.[21] This had been visited two years before by the Inspector General of the Air Raid Precautions Department and assessed as being, in some regards, safer from air attack then the castle as it was much less identifiable from the air.[22] Under the care of their governess, the princesses received dancing classes led by Betty Vacani, a famous London dancing mistress, and Elizabeth had history lessons at Eton with Marten while the King and Queen came to visit at weekends. This lasted until 12 May when the Queen telephoned Crawfie, as she was called by the Royal Family, and told her to take the two girls to the castle "at least for the rest of the week".[23] They ended up staying at Windsor, described as "a fortress, not a home", for most of the rest of the war.[24]

Whilst the established Royal residences had been sufficient during the period commonly referred to as 'The Phoney War', when there seemed no immediate threat to the safety of the King and Queen and their daughters, preparations were underway elsewhere for if this no longer proved the case. One of those who was directly involved has provided details of what was done to make ready a

---

17 Ben Pimlott, *The Queen – A Biography of Elizabeth II* (London; Harper Collins Publishers, 1997), p.56-57; Shawcross, *Queen Elizabeth*, p.495; Minute by Chief Inspector, 4 September 1939, MEPO3/1898, TNA

18 Although close to the family during this period, having worked for them since 1930, her post-war publication of an autobiographical account of her time acting as governess to the princesses led to her being ostracised; Vanessa Thorpe, 'Queen Mother was "ruthless" to royal nanny', *The Observer*, 25 June 2000

19 Robert Lacey, *Majesty – Elizabeth II and the House of Windsor* (London; Hutchinson of London, 1977), p.136

20 Marion Crawford, *The Little Princesses* (London; Orion, 2003), pp.105-115

21 Ellen Couzens, "The Queen's War" – Queen Elizabeth II During WW2' (Blog), 10 February 2013, http://royalcentral.co.uk/blogs/the-queens-war-queen-elizabeth-ii-during-ww2-2773

22 C.L. Stocks to Major Sir Ulick Alexander, 18 January 1938, CRES46/35, TNA

23 Bradford, *Elizabeth*, p.90; Crawford, *The Little Princesses*, p.199; according to the police report they were in residence from 10 May 1940

24 Crawford, *The Little Princesses*, pp.69, 119

contingency if the worst were to happen.[25] Frederick Corbitt, who would go on to become Deputy Comptroller of Supply at Buckingham Palace, was only 28 years of age when the war broke out and a junior member of staff. In his post-career memoir he details the story of being summoned soon after the outbreak by "a very high official of the Court" and being given personal orders for a "special security job" that came from the King himself. At this time he was told of the existence of a large mansion in the West Country which was referred to as 'Establishment "A"' and which he was informed was to be prepared as a refuge in the event of the Royal Family being forced to leave London. As part of his duties he visited the unnamed property early in 1940 where he stayed for two days and nights and looked around the neighbouring "quiet little village" and the surrounding countryside in order to confirm what shopping facilities there were to supply the possible future tenants. The purpose of his visit was kept a secret even from his wife and the only people who knew why he was in Worcestershire were the owners, who he referred to as "a man of title", and his wife. Corbitt did later write that during his visit he met the local butcher, poulterer and fishmonger explaining to them that he might be returning with "some VIPs ... at some distant date without much advance notice"; they were all "staggered" as he also went on to describe the possible food orders he would be placing.[26] He was joined by Mrs Fergusson, the Royal Housekeeper from the Palace, who was there to check on final arrangements "for the comfort of the staff and the suite". In advance of his visit emergency stores supplied by a London grocery firm had been sent down addressed to Corbitt. A large quantity of bedding, mattresses and furniture had also been sent from Windsor Castle by lorry for use in the staff quarters. These were supposed to be marked with the 'Establishment "A"' tag but instead they all bore large yellow labels stamped with a black crown and the words 'Royal Mews' in black lettering; this featured in a report he wrote in which he confirmed that plans were now in readiness for the evacuation. At this time those members of the Royal Household who would be involved in the move were told the part that they were to play and sworn to secrecy although as the author put it "it seemed to many of us, including myself, to be just another rather silly precaution".[27]

There are some issues relating to this account. Certainly one of the few accounts of life at Croome during this period, written by Lady Coventry's personal maid, makes no reference to any visit or the potential secret role.[28] There is also some doubt about who Corbitt might have met. At the outbreak of war Lord Coventry had enlisted and become Lieutenant George Coventry, 7th Battalion, Worcestershire Regiment, while Lady Coventry also joined up and became the

25 F.J. Corbitt, *My Twenty Years in Buckingham Palace – A Book of Intimate Memoirs* (New York; David McKay Company Inc., 1956), pp.158-162
26 Ibid., p.159
27 Ibid., p.160
28 Newman, *Diamonds at Dinner*

County Commandant for Worcestershire in the Auxiliary Territorial Service.[29] It is not impossible that he might have returned home for such an important visit but no records exist; aged just 39 years old, he was killed on 27 May 1940 during the evacuation of British forces from Dunkirk. Three weeks before, whether it was because of the security lapse or some other reason, Lord and Lady Coventry had been informed that Croome would no longer be needed and a house more conveniently placed was to be instead used.[30] The Office of Works now took over the requisitioned tenancy of his home and from August 1940 to the following August the Dutch government were sub-tenants although the property was never actually used by Queen Wilhelmina, who preferred to stay with Prince Bernhard in a property in Eaton Square in central London.[31] It was also reportedly one of the sites selected for Queen Mary, the King's mother who had been evacuated to Badminton House at the start of the war, as a secondary refuge should an invasion force her to flee further north. Its eventual main wartime role was even more unusual. With its vast grounds work had also started at Croome in 1939 – another account refers to the following year – to construct RAF Defford and three years later this became the home for the Telecommunications Flying Unit which played a vital role in the development of radar.[32] Whether it was Croome or not, Corbitt returned in 1944 to the mansion he had first visited four years before to recover the stores that had been transferred there during the war's early months. He found that virtually all the tinned goods were still in excellent condition although "the large jars of turtle soup and turtle meat which had been included for use at the Royal table had gone bad".[33] These were thrown away along with the now sticky bags of lump sugar but everything else was packed up and returned to London.

It seems clear that, in realising, the months prior to the surrender of France in June 1940 had been marked by a lack of urgency in terms of making any detailed plans for how to respond to the potential danger facing the Royal Family. This was quickly about to change as Britain faced up the threat of attack from the air and invasion by sea and land. And as events quickly demonstrated there was every reason to believe that the King and Queen would be centrally involved in what was to follow.

29 Ibid., pp.231-234, 248; 'Obituary – The Earl of Coventry', *Daily Telegraph*, 21 June 2002
30 Research by Richard Beighton; Tovey, 'The role of Croome Court during WW2...'
31 Correspondence with Hickson, 11 January 2011
32 The Friends of Croome Park, *Croome before the National Trust* (Stoke-on-Trent; Wood Mitchell Printers Ltd, 2014), pp.10-11; Newman, *Diamonds at Dinner*, pp.250-251
33 Corbitt, *My Twenty Years in Buckingham Palace*, p.161

2

The Bomber Always Gets Through

With the outbreak of the war it was clear that at the outset the greatest concern for the Royal Family's safety lay with the potential threat from the air. As far back as 1925 an inter-service committee had been established to consider future air-raid precautions. As part of this study the Air Ministry was asked to provide an estimate, based upon what were later judged to be questionable statistics and with the French air forces viewed as the likely threat, of what the level of destruction would be in the event of an attack on London. This calculated that 1700 people would be killed and 3300 injured in the first 24 hours alone, a rate which after the first two days would halve but then remain constant. This meant that in the first three days of the next air war it was assumed that losses would be twice those for the entire country during the First World War. Despite the War Office challenging the figures and the narrative they presented, the Air Ministry refused to alter them or the conclusion that there was no defence possible against this level of attack.[1] As the noted air historian John Terraine described it, "this was the start of that tenacious theory of the 'knock-out blow'" and the British inter-war prime minister Stanley Baldwin's alleged comment that "the bomber will always get through".[2] This sentiment certainly prevailed in the October 1936 report produced by the Joint Planning Committee of the Chiefs of Staff which examined the probable course of a fictional war starting three years later.[3] This highlighted the now much enhanced destructive potential of a German air offensive and calculated that there would be 150,000 casualties within the first week leaving "angry and frightened mobs of civilians", threatening the complete collapse of civil society. The reality was very different: before the Munich crisis of September 1938, at which stage there were no fighters that had the range to escort the *Luftwaffe*'s bombers, there had actually been no German planning for any aerial attack on London. The British military planners appeared to be unaware of such facts and this drove them forward in anticipating a catastrophic initial phase of the next war, a process which extended to the Royal Family.[4]

1 John Terraine, *The Right of the Line: the Royal Air Force in the European War, 1939-1945* (London; Hodder and Stoughton, 1985), p.11
2 Ibid., p.12
3 Ibid., p.49
4 Ibid., pp.55-59; Brian Bond, *British Military Policy between the Two World Wars* (Oxford; Clarendon Press, 1980), p.283

At Windsor preparations were made: pictures were moved into the cellars; glass-fronted cupboards were emptied of their displays and turned towards the walls; the glass chandeliers were taken down because of the danger they could cause as splinters and the State Apartments were covered in dust sheets. Aside from the blacking out of all the windows the high-powered bulbs were also replaced with lower powered substitutes to conform with the ARP regulations, which "created a sepulchral gloom".[5] More long-lasting steps were also taken most notably with a large dugout being constructed at the northern corner of the East Terrace to act as a deep underground shelter.[6] Both the King and Queen disliked this "hole in the ground" which was at some distance from their main rooms and from September 1940 they usually slept on the ground floor in the Victoria Tower.[7] Now the Queen's Tower, this had been given additional protection with huge concrete frames which were filled with sand along with a 10 inch concrete, steel and asbestos raft across the roof. There had also been four feet of concrete and girders placed on the floor which provided an extra layer of protection for the four rooms in the cellar, and where they were able to sleep immune to everything except dive bombers. Following their arrival the two princesses initially had slept in the dungeons as the air raid shelter was under the Brunswick Tower although they later returned to their usual rooms in the Lancaster Tower, three storeys high and dating from Henry VII's reign. A combination of sirens outside the building and loud electric bells inside ensured that those within the castle received ample warning of impending air raids from the watchers on the roof. When a red warning was given and a special bell rang, meaning that aircraft were flying directly overhead, the princesses were taken down to the shelter.[8] The first siren sounded within two days of their arrival and it took some time before Elizabeth and Margaret were escorted to the shelter as their nanny struggled to dress them. The situation improved in part because the two girls were given siren suits to wear and little suitcases in which they kept their dolls, books and treasures and their exit to the shelters became well practiced.[9]

The castle also became a temporary home to other precious items. Plans had begun in September 1938 to evacuate art from Buckingham Palace and a total of 57 valuable pictures were identified by Sir Kenneth Clark, the Surveyor of the King's Pictures, to be moved to Windsor or elsewhere.[10] In correspondence about the potential movement of art treasures Brigadier-General Sir Smith Hill

5   Lacey, *Majesty*, p.143
6   Shawcross, *Queen Elizabeth*, p.527; Pimlott, *The Queen*, p.57. Work had also been carried out at the Royal Lodge the result of which was an air-conditioned shelter, possibly why the Princesses spent time there during 1940; Ulick Alexander to E.H. Savill, 18 September 1940, CRES46/35, TNA
7   Shawcross, *Queen Elizabeth*, p.527
8   Crawford, *The Little Princesses*, pp.119-125
9   Lacey, *Majesty*, p.143
10 F.P. Robinson to E.N. de Normann, 22 September 1938, WORK28/20, TNA; ibid., Minute by de Normann, 22 September 1938

Child had written that "I don't imagine the Royal residences would be specially selected for bombing, but if they were, Windsor Castle on the bank of the river would be a very tempting target".[11] One of the most influential figures in helping make arrangements for the Royal Family's protection, Hill Child, the Master of the Household, had been born in September 1880 and had a background which included Eton, Oxford and the Irish Guards although he received his wartime DSO for commanding an artillery division. After a term as a Member of Parliament he entered the Royal Household in 1927, served as Master until 1941 and was still serving as an extra Equerry to the Queen in November 1958 when he died.[12] A lorry was eventually provided by the Ministry of Works with another being set aside to transport china. There was, however, some debate about where it should be sent and whilst some items almost certainly went to Windsor many appear to have been kept in central London; with the Aldwych and Dover Street Tube station earmarked for British Museum and the Victoria and Albert pieces it was eventually decided that storage at Knightsbridge Tube would be used.[13] There was allegedly also something else to protect at Windsor. According to Crawfie she was taken down into the vaults one day by Sir Owen Morshead, the King's Librarian, who showed her "a lot of rather ordinary looking leather hat boxes" which when examined revealed the Crown Jewels hidden in them.[14] In his own account he recorded that it had been under the King's direction that they had been moved in unmarked cars overseen by Gerrards, the Royal jewellers, which had taken them in specially padded boxes from the Tower of London. They had been met at Windsor by Morshead and the King and the items were taken inside where the two of them used pliers supplied by the latter's chauffeurs "to wrench the major gems off their settings in the crowns". This included the fabulous Koh-i-noor diamond which, along with the others, was wrapped in cotton wool and put in the hatboxes that Crawfie was later shown.

Arrangements at Buckingham Palace were not nearly so well organised and the results were not the "virtually impregnable redoubt" that some have claimed.[15] In February 1938 the buildings had been surveyed by the Office of Works and this indicated that the solid construction could withstand aerial attack with suitable accommodation in the basement for about 300 people, although there were some fears that the palace roof would not withstand incendiary bombs.[16] For the Royal Family a special shelter would, however, need to be constructed, and the

11   Ibid., Hill Child to Sir Patrick Duff, 14 October 1938
12   'Obituary – Sir Hill Child', *The Times*, November 12, 1958
13   Minute by de Normann, 29 December 1938, WORKS28/20, TNA; ibid., Minute by LWB, 29 August 1939
14   Crawford, *The Little Princesses*, p.127; Sir Owen Morshead, *Windsor Castle* (London; Phaidon Press Ltd., 1971); Leo McKinstry, *Operation Sealion: How Britain Crushed the German War Machine's Dream of Invasion in 1940* (London; John Murray, 2014), p.233
15   Philip Ziegler, *London at War 1939-1945* (London; Pimlico, 2002), pp.24-25
16   Patrick Duff to Wing Commander E.J. Hodsoll, 1 March 1938, WORK19/799, TNA

considerable cost along with the publicity that would be involved in building something under the terrace on the north front was a cause for some unease. In the short term the housemaids' basement sitting-room was reinforced and fitted out with baskets of sand, hand-pumps and emergency stairs. There were some steel supports added along with wooden partitions to provide a degree of privacy for those forced to spend time underground.[17] For the first part of the German aerial onslaught this "somewhat amateurish" setup, one that was much disliked by the Queen, served as the Royal air raid shelter in central London.[18] In the rooms nearby the remainder of the Household also took shelter along with those priceless articles from the main building which had not been moved elsewhere. It had been hoped that in the event of an emergency they would be evacuated at once to Windsor, a view which also received considerable support from within the Home Office.[19] Cost was a very real consideration in all of the discussions about building shelters at Royal residences as expenditure on property not considered to be within the remit of the 'Royal Palaces' presented something of a challenge. As the Keeper of the Privy Purse, Major Sir Ulick Alexander, pointed out "the question of the King's life in time of war should be considered as a charge against public funds"; hence, even in the case of Balmoral which was a private residence it seems that the government was prepared to pay the estimated £1500 to construct a bomb proof dugout.[20]

These preparations proved to be farsighted and of vital importance. Buckingham Palace was eventually bombed on a total of sixteen occasions throughout the war and received nine direct hits. In January 1940 the London Fire Brigade had inspected the lake in the gardens to check how easy it would be to draw water from it to tackle fires in the wider area, but eventually it was agreed that it would be reserved for just that building.[21] This was soon put into effect when the first of the attacks on the Royal Family's London home took place on 8 September 1940, a Sunday evening and the second night of heavy bombing that formed part of the so-called 'Blitz' during which the capital was attacked on 57 consecutive days or nights. By mid-November over 13,000 tons of high explosives and nearly one million incendiaries had been dropped on London; across the entire country the figure for the year was 37,000 tons suggesting that the planners had not been entirely misplaced in their gloomy assessments.[22] During this first attack on the

17 Cadbury, *Princes at War*, p.165
18 Wheeler-Bennett, *King George VI*, pp.462-463; Shawcross, *Queen Elizabeth*, p.517-518; Theo Aronson, *The Royal Family at War* (London; John Murray, 1994), pp.28-29. Aronson "was a royal biographer with an easy manner which enabled him to meet and earn the trust of his subjects"; 'Obituary: Theo Aronson', Daily Telegraph (London), 15 May 2003
19 Hodsoll to Duff, 4 March 1938, WORK19/799, TNA; ibid., Hodsoll to Duff, 22 March 1938
20 Ibid., Ulick Alexander to Sir Warren Fisher, 11 May 1939
21 Jackson (London Fire Brigade Headquarters) to Macintyre (Office of Works), 30 November 1939, HO209/1, TNA; ibid., Macintrye to Jackson, 26 December 1939; Home Office minute, 14 February 1940
22 Richard Holmes, *Churchill's Bunker: The Secret Headquarters at the Heart of Britain's Victory*

Following the attack on 13 September 1940 two large craters were left in the internal courtyard. The King and Queen subsequently inspected the damage and spoke with some of the men removing the debris. German official broadcasts claimed that Winston Churchill had placed the bombs there to deliberately manipulate British public opinion.

Palace approximately 200 German bombers flew over central London dropping incendiaries and explosives around Westminster; one of these, a delayed-action bomb, landed harmlessly in the grounds.[23]

The following day a second bomb fell close to a swimming pool that had been built two years before for the princesses in a former conservatory at the north western part of the Palace on the West Terrace. This lodged itself under the stone steps outside the Regency Room and close to the Queen's dressing-room and bathroom and near the King's study. It failed to explode and, with the sounding of the 'All Clear', the King initially continued using his working room before setting out for a tour of the east of the city to view the damage. Attempts were made by Sappers from the Royal Engineers to remove the bomb and they dug throughout the day in an attempt to reach it but it was well buried and eventually exploded the next day in the early hours of the Tuesday morning.[24] Every

(London; Profile Books, 2011), p.219

23 William Sansom, *The Blitz: Westminster at War* (Oxford; Oxford University Press, 1990), p.29. With full co-operation from the Home Office this was first published in 1947 as an account of the role played by the Civil Defence organisation

24 Ibid., p.41

View showing the section of railings that were destroyed.

window in the Palace had been covered in wire netting but those in the north front were broken on every floor, doors were blown off and plaster dislodged from the ceilings. The main structure remained intact aside from some damage to the roof caused by several heavy pieces of Portland stone that had been scattered by the blast as much as 300 feet into the air. The swimming pool was badly damaged, "the diving stand … leans sideways, twisted and torn" and in what water remained "there floated melancholy wreckage, unshapely pieces of timber snapped from here and there by the relentless blast"; it was not rebuilt until the war's end.[25] No injuries were caused as all of the Household staff were in the basement shelters. The Times noted that "as elsewhere in the Palace, all the treasures has long since been removed from this choice room to a place of greater safety".[26] The Prime Minister joined the King and Queen for lunch on the Tuesday and, together, they inspected the damage.

25 'Heavy Bomb on the Palace', The Times, September 12, 1940; Claudia Joseph, 'From Philip's daily dips to Charles's childhood boat races and now George's first swimming lessons, a peek inside the most exclusive paddling pool in Britain! Daily Mail, 11 August 2014
26 'Heavy Bomb…', The Times, September 12, 1940

The small Royal Chapel in the South Wing of Buckingham Palace which was struck by a German bomb on 13 September 1940 (picture taken after the attack).

View of the chapel before the attack. This was where the two princesses had been christened; the famous Gobelins tapestry and Queen Alexandra's family Bible had both been removed prior to the attack.

Much more serious was the attack on Friday 13 September 1940 when a single German bomber flew straight up the Mall and dropped six bombs.[27] The weather was unsettled and it was a cloudy and rainy morning when at about 11am, and with no aircraft from the RAF operating due to the conditions, the single raider dropped in below the clouds and the barrage balloons.[28] As one account put it "his intentions were undoubted, his aim was good – but the results finally less fortunate for the *Luftwaffe* than for England".[29] It was actually one of two bombers that attacked London from different directions; the other reportedly dropped its bombs on Whitehall and part of Downing Street although there was no reference to this in the minutes of the War Cabinet meeting which had also started at 11am and was interrupted with the news that the Palace had been attacked.[30] The King, who was working in his little sitting-room overlooking the inner quadrangle, heard the approach before the aircraft shut off its engines as it passed overhead.[31] Two bombs hit the red gravel only 30 yards away from him and as he wrote in his diary, "we went to London and found an Air Raid in progress. The day was very cloudy and it was raining hard. We were both upstairs with Alec Hardinge talking in my little sitting room overlooking the quadrangle; (I cannot use my ordinary one owing to the broken windows) … All of a sudden we heard an aircraft making a zooming noise above us, saw two bombs falling past the opposite side of the Palace, and then heard two resounding crashes as the bombs fell in the quadrangle about 30 yards away. We looked at each other, and then we were out into the passage as fast as we could get there. The whole thing happened in a matter of seconds. We all wondered why we weren't dead".[32] A private letter written by Queen Elizabeth to her mother-in-law Queen Mary later in the day and only made public in 2009 provides an even more detailed account of what happened.[33] Despite their being a 'Red' warning the King had gone up to "our poor windowless rooms to collect a few odds and ends" and had paused to ask his wife to remove an eyelash from his eye. Hardinge joined them at which point there was "the noise of an aircraft diving at great speed, and then the scream of a bomb". With no time to move until after "a tremendous crash in the quadrangle"

27 The contemporary account referred to this total but those written later lowered the number; 'Damage by Bombs at the Palace', *The Times*, September 16, 1940
28 'Operations Record Book – 504 Squadron', 13 September 1940, AIR27/1964, TNA
29 Sansom, *The Blitz*, pp.35-36
30 It was immediately agreed to send the message, "The War Cabinet offer their hearty congratulations to their Majesties on their providential escape from the barbarous attack made on their home and Royal Persons"; War Cabinet Meeting 249(40), 13 September 1940, CAB65/9/11, TNA
31 'Buckingham Palace again Bombed', *The Times*, September 14, 1940; ibid., 'Bombs on Downing Street'
32 Wheeler-Bennett, *King George VI*, p.468; Sir Alan Lascelles to Winston Churchill, 28 April 1948, Churchill Papers, Churchill Archives Centre, CHUR 4/201A (hereafter 'CAC')
33 Caroline Davies, 'How the Luftwaffe bombed the palace, in the Queen Mother's own words', *The Guardian*, 13 September 2009; Queen Elizabeth to Queen Mary, 13 September 1940, The Royal Archives, Windsor, http://www.royalcollection.org.uk/exhibitions/letter-from-queen-elizabeth-to-queen-mary-describing-the-bombing-of-buckingham-palace-13

the three then "ducked like lightning into the corridor" where they had to pause with two pages as there was another tremendous explosion. They waited away from the staircase in case of flying glass before proceeding to the shelter. As she went to check on the housemaids in their adjacent shelter the Queen noted that everybody "remained wonderfully calm" although she did later admit that "my knees trembled a little bit for a minute or two after the explosions!". But, as she concluded her letter, "Dear old B.P. is still standing and that is the main thing".

The most obvious results of the attack were two large craters in the inner quadrangle and the resulting explosions burst a fire hydrant causing a fountain of water ten feet high. This poured through the broken windows on the southern and western sides, where the ground floor Ambassadors' Corridor and the tall portraits hanging there had been badly damaged. In the pillared Grand Entrance "debris covered the crimson carpet, and a light dust clouded the white walls with its gilded decorations".[34] Considerable damage was caused by a third bomb which struck the small Royal Chapel in the South Wing and four men in the plumber's workshop below had a narrow escape although one later died from his injuries.[35] Only a small hole was visible in the roof where the bomb had entered the chapel but inside there was total destruction, "a heavy alabaster pulpit with broken, the organ damaged, a fine tapestry thrown down from behind the altar: only the iron columns, tipped with their gold Corinthian capitals, stood firm above the wreckage of sacred ornament and life".[36] Finally, two delayed-action bombs fell on the forecourt and on the roadway between the Palace gates and the Victoria Memorial. An officer from the Rescue Service volunteered to build a sandbag wall around one of these bombs which threatened the Palace's façade and a team of volunteers formed to help manhandle the required 'building blocks'; a barrier five feet thick and six feet high was built in the hours that followed. The eventual explosion the following morning created a ten foot deep crater but only demolished a section of railings and showered the Victoria Memorial with debris; the man who had led the operation to save the Palace was later awarded the George Medal for his work.[37] It seemed clear to those who had witnessed it that this had been deliberate, the Palace superintendent was quoted as saying that "he heard a terrific rushing noise and saw a German aeroplane come down to about 1000 feet through the balloon barrage" before watching it make a direct line for the Palace.[38] As the King wrote "there is no doubt that it was a direct attack on Buckingham Palace" and it was suspected it might have been carried out by

34 Sansom, *The Blitz*, p.36
35 The initial press report was of three injuries none of which had been serious; 'Buckingham Palace again Bombed', *The Times*, September 14, 1940
36 Sansom, *The Blitz*, p.36
37 Ibid., p.37
38 'Damage by Bombs…', *The Times*, September 16, 1940

somebody who had a detailed knowledge of the target, possibly one of his many German relations.[39]

There was another attack still to come on the following Sunday, which was also subsequently referred to as 'Battle of Britain Day' and marked the culmination of the daytime fighter battles.[40] An intense fight developed between German and British aircraft over central London at around noon involving nearly 100 aircraft and towards its conclusion a German bomber along with a Hurricane fighter crashed on the streets below. As the daily intelligence report for No.504 Squadron noted, "A Do[rnier] 215 attacked by Sergeant Holmes apparently exploded in the air directly beneath him causing his Hurricane to go down in an uncontrollable spin and forcing him to bale out".[41] In what was one of the most celebrated events of the air battles that took place throughout 1940, it was later determined that the 26 year old Sergeant Ray 'Arty' Holmes, having run out of ammunition, had pursued and rammed the damaged German aircraft which crashed into the forecourt of Victoria Station, one of 60 aircraft to be lost by the *Luftwaffe* that day.[42] Before its final destruction the Dornier, piloted by Hauptmann Ernst Püttmann who, along with the rest of the crew was killed in the crash, managed to drop two bombs one which landed on the lawn of Buckingham Palace with the other hitting the Regency bathroom overlooking the West Terrace. This second bomb, about 50 kilos in weight, was found lying on the green carpet alongside the bath in the unoccupied Belgian Suite reserved normally for foreign guests. As one account put it, it was reported by Palace servants and an officer from the Royal Engineers quickly arrived and "took it up on his shoulder, and carried it over the green carpet, out through the French windows, on to the stone terrace and thence to the lawn, where he dumped it temporarily under a tree". Later that afternoon this and another bomb were taken by lorry down to the lake at the far end of the gardens and blown up.[43] No evidence has ever been established whether this was a deliberate attack, or the crew of a crippled aircraft using their final moments to attack an obvious target.

The German bombs continued to fall and another raid on 1 November saw one land on the lawn about 40 yards away from the western front of the Palace

39 The principal suspect was Prince Christoph of Hesse, an officer in the Luftwaffe, but investigations into who might have been responsible appeared to exonerate him and the other likely candidate, a son of Don Alfonso of Spain, although he may have been involved in the planning; Bradford, *Elizabeth*, p.324; Hugo Vickers, *Elizabeth – The Queen Mother* (London; Hutchinson, 2005), p.217; Jonathan Petropoulos, *Royals and the Reich: The Princes von Hessen in Nazi Germany* (Oxford; Oxford University Press, 2009), pp.229-231

40 Roy Jenkins, *Churchill* (London; Macmillan, 2001), p.633; Fleming, *Invasion 1940*, p.134

41 'Intelligence Patrol Report – No.504 Squadron, 1123-1255 hrs, 15.9.40', AIR50/163, TNA; Francis K. Mason, *Battle over Britain* (London; McWhirter Twins Ltd., 1969), pp.388, 393

42 Ronan Thomas, 'Sgt Ray Holmes – Hurricane Pilot', *West End at War*, http://www.westendatwar. org.uk/page_id__146.aspx; 'Pilot who "saved Palace" honoured', *BBC News*, 2 November 2005, http://news.bbc.co.uk/1/hi/england/leicestershire/4398484.stm

43 Sansom, *The Blitz*, pp.40-41; 'Damage Appreciation – Key Points Intelligence Branch', 16 September 1940, HO201/2, TNA

The ten foot deep crater that was produced by the two delayed-action bombs which exploded the following morning. As a result of the efforts of the Rescue Service who laboured through the night to build a sandbag wall these only demolished a section of railings and showered the Victoria Memorial with debris.

Whilst it was very well received by the British public, there were some concerns about the danger the King and Queen exposed themselves to in visiting Londoners who had been bombed out of their homes.

leading to an explosion which smashed windows and caused some damage to the Riding School.[44] In the following weeks there were further minor incidents involving incendiaries which were dealt with by the Palace's fire brigade, and some further minor damage was caused by stray rounds of ammunition, both British and German. The next serious raid was the following year, a brightly moonlit Saturday night when the North Lodge was destroyed by single bomb. This attack on 8 March 1941 caused considerable damage and resulted in the death of one police constable who had been on patrol in the forecourt when the bomb struck. Later that evening a further stick of seven bombs fell in line straddling the Palace and caused some additional blast damage to the front of the building.[45] Ultimately this landmark survived the war but not without some serious scars, one writer later noting that, "glass was out of the windows, and in its place appeared grey boarding that gave the great façades an empty look, as though blinds had been drawn for some endless summer vacation. A section of the tall front railings was replaced by a series of smaller temporary shafts. The high ivied brick wall skirting Constitution Hill became breached with corrugated iron. In the daily life of the forecourt there was no longer the scarlet changing of the guard. Conical armoured sentry-boxes stood by the gates, and Bren gun carriers rumbled out of William IV's grey Wellington Barracks nearby".[46]

Windsor was not spared and in October it was attacked on two consecutive nights although the castle was not hit; prior to this, on 30 September, a Messerschmitt 109 fighter was shot down in Windsor Great Park. In order to provide better protection against future air attacks a number of three-inch anti-aircraft guns were now placed in the vicinity of the Castle at Datchet and Dorney Common. In January 1941, and after considerable discussion, these were changed for larger calibre weapons despite there being considerable demands elsewhere for these powerful 3.7 inch guns, an indication of the level of threat that was felt to exist.[47] From October 1940 onwards with the remaining regimental horses having been sent to Melton Mowbray for the duration of the war, anti-para-chute patrols of the Great Park were conducted on bicycles at dawn and dusk with the Troop Leader conducting his duties in an Austin '7'. There were also dismounted positions to man the reservoirs at Staines and Laleham to prevent German seaplanes landing on them, and a few ancient Hotchkiss guns were issued from Woolwich to the defenders.[48] In addition a total of seven pillboxes with accompanying barbed wire defences were constructed on Crown Lands, one of which was near Queen Anne's Gate and another near the entrance to

44 Sansom, *The Blitz*, p.42
45 Ibid.
46 Ibid., p.43
47 Hastings Ismay to Lord Wigram, 4 December 1940, CAB21/1095, TNA
48 Julian Paget, *The Story of the Guards* (London; Michael Joseph Ltd., 1979), pp.191-192; Roden Orde, *The Household Cavalry at War: Second Household Cavalry Regiment* (Aldershot; Gale and Polden Ltd., 1953), pp.5-6

The King and Queen made a number of visits "to see things for themselves" as one contemporary magazine wrote; here they are inspecting deep shelters in the East End of London.

On 14 November 1940 the city of Coventry was attacked by more than 500 German aircraft killing an estimated 568 people and seriously injuring more than 800 others in what was once of the worst air attacks outside of London. The following day the King visited and it was recorded that "in swelling volume the crowd began to sing the National Anthem".

the Royal Lodge.[49] With this understandable focus on local security it was perhaps surprising that, following an attack on the company's aircraft factory at Weybridge, it was proposed in November 1940 that an aerodrome would be constructed by Vickers Armstrong on Smith's Lawn in Windsor Great Park to be used for the construction of Wellington bombers.[50] This idea was examined by the Chiefs of Staff Committee where the concerns of the Home Secretary were noted about what risk this might constitute to the King's safety.[51] The conclusion was that this proposed site would not represent any threat to the castle or its occupants and would provide no additional landmark for German bombers.[52] Approval was consequently given and two brick hangers were built, one situated near the road that comes in from Cheesemans Gate where fuselage sections were built; a total of 64 Wellington Mark VIs were assembled on Smith's Lawn at the site which had an east-west grass unlit runway which was camouflaged and dummy hay stacks and canvas lorries.[53]

One influential writer has argued that the King's 'narrow escape' during the bombing of Buckingham Palace was "a stroke of luck" that could not have come "at a more opportune moment".[54] This argument proposes that there was only conditional support for the Royal Family at this stage in the war but the situation improved following the perceived attacks on them. According to the conclusions of the Mass Observation monitors, the King was seen as "a symbol of the country" and these helped forge a new bond with his people as "Buckingham Palace had been bombed as well as their homes, and nothing is immune".[55] Ministry of Information daily morale reports, in fact, suggested that public support for the sovereign was never higher, the only concern being that unnecessary risks were being taken with the visits to bomb damaged areas.[56] An exception to this appeared to come from the *Daily Worker* which highlighted how the British media had used the story as "a golden opportunity to unload the 'unity of the classes' and 'their home as well as yours' stuff" and this newspaper remained more interested in the numerous other "castles and palaces" in the which the Royal Family could take shelter.[57]

In reality the bombing clearly had a huge propaganda effect and undoubtedly produced a wave of sympathy towards the Royal Family as was illustrated by

---

49 Minute, 21 September 1940, CRES46/46, TNA
50 Smith's Lawn is the site today of the Guards Polo Club but from the 1920s there had been a grass airstrip at the site; Minute to Secretary of State, 25 November 1940, CAB121/227, TNA
51 Ibid., 'Extract from COS (40)369 Meeting', 27 November 1940
52 Ibid., L.G. Hollis to Norman Brooke, 29 November 1940
53 Clifford Smith, *The Great Park and Windsor Forest* (Windsor; Bank House Books, 2004)
54 Andrew Roberts, *Eminent Churchillians* (London; Weidenfeld and Nicolson, 1994), p.49
55 Ibid., p.51
56 'Saturday 14 September 1940', in Paul Addison and Jeremy A. Crang (eds.), *Listening to Britain: Home Intelligence Reports on Britain's Finest Hour – May to September 1940* (London; The Bodley Head, 2010), pp.420-421
57 William Rust, '"A stimulating effect on the people"', *Daily Worker*, Tuesday, September 17, 1940

cinemagoers cheering coverage of the King and Queen walking calmly through the destroyed streets of London.[58] The Queen famously believed this attack meant that she could "look the East End in the face" which is exactly what she did later in the afternoon of 13 September as she and her husband toured a bombed out area.[59] Photographs of the damage were published around the world and the attacks were covered at home although in some cases with a delay of several days in the publication; the proximity of the first bomb to the King was not made public even to Churchill until after the war.[60] It was, however, made clear that the Palace had been damaged with a party of 40 journalists being taken around the ruins the same day by the King's Assistant Private Secretary Alan Lascelles. According to the *National Review*, despite there being no mistaking that the German intention had been their murder, "the Royal routine was not even halted for half an hour".[61] The Canadian Minister of Munitions and Supply, C.D. Howe, had set off in mid-December 1940 to visit Britain but was torpedoed and forced to spend nine hours in a lifeboat before he was rescued. He was granted an hour long audience with the King when he eventually arrived, and as he noted in his diary, "practically all the windows in Buckingham Palace have been broken, and the room in which His Majesty received me had beaver board in the windows instead of glass. His Majesty said that he had moved his office three times and had finally decided to stay where he was for the duration".[62]

Messages of support were received from all around the Empire praising the Royal Family's courage and expressing anger at the attack that had been carried out against them. Typical was that from Sierra Leone and its assurance that "such acts of frightfulness only serve to confirm the purpose of this ancient and loyal Colony to prosecute the war with the utmost vigour".[63] Speaking in the House of Parliament, Churchill told those assembled that the attacks and their "general barbarity" had been designed to "have an unsettling effect upon public opinion". They had failed to do so and had instead united "the King and Queen to their

58 Denis Judd, 'George VI – The everyman king', *BBC History Magazine* (Vol.13, No.1; January 2012), pp.22-23; Addison and Crang (eds.), *Listening to Britain*, p.435; Ziegler, *London at War 1939-1945*, p.121

59 Wheeler-Bennett, *King George VI*, pp.469-470; Sarah Bradford, *The Reluctant King – The Life and Reign of George VI 1895-1952* (New York; St Martin's Press, 1990), p.325; Shawcross, *Queen Elizabeth*, p.526; Crawford, *The Little Princesses*, pp.145-146; Corbitt, *My Twenty Years in Buckingham Palace*, pp.145-148

60 'Damage by Bombs…', *The Times*, September 16, 1940; ''Dive bombers try to kill the King and Queen', *Daily Express*, Saturday, September 14, 1940; ibid., 'Hitler's murder mission: U.S. rage at Palace bombing'

61 Letter from Tommy Lascelles to Joan Thesiger, 11 September 1940, Lascelles Papers (Churchill Archives Centre) LASL II, 1/19; 'The Attack on the King and Queen', *National Review (incorporating The English Review)* (Vol.CXV, July to December 1940), p.378

62 Diary, 23 December 1940, C.D. Howe Papers (Library Archives of Canada, Ottawa), MG27 III, B20, Vol.192

63 'Empire's Pride in the King and Queen', *The Times*, September 17, 1940; ibid., 'Bombs on the Palace', September 18, 1940

people by new and sacred bonds of common danger, and they steel the hearts of all to the stern and unrelenting prosecution of the war against so foul a foe".[64] Having first denied the attacks, in response German broadcasting stations reported that the Palace was near Wellington Barracks and Victoria Station and "important oil tanks" and it was difficult to discriminate between military and non-military targets.[65] This apparent justification was quickly changed and various newspapers appeared to describe the raids as retaliation for the bombing of German towns.[66]

The King remained concerned about the threat from the air and asked if the distinctive nature of the Queen Victoria Memorial in front of Buckingham Palace had provided assistance to the German pilots who had attacked his London home.[67] It had previously been recommended that no buildings or monuments needed to be removed and there was no need to drain either the Serpentine or the lake in St James's Park. In June 1941 a reconnaissance flight by a RAF Group Captain confirmed that these were not providing a guide to the attackers. The subsequent report noted that if the enemy were using any ground features it would have been the Thames along with a combination of the Royal Parks acting as markers. Flying at a height of 15,000 feet with a three-quarter moon he also noted, however, that no individual buildings could be viewed and it was "a matter of chance" as to whether the lakes that were scattered around the parks could be seen or not; the conclusion was that "one could only guess where the Palace was".

Shortly afterwards in September 1941, and with the worst of the Blitz over, further thought was given to providing suitable reinforced accommodation for the Royal Family. A variety of schemes were now proposed including additional work at Buckingham Palace and the provision of part of the shelter at Down Street that was used by the Prime Minister. After two months of discussions it was agreed that a flat at Curzon Street would be made available; Curzon Street House had been requisitioned at the beginning of the war and was considered as a 'citadel' available for essential staff from the service departments to continue work during periods of bombing.[68] A fully furnished flat on the fourth floor with nine rooms for the monarch plus staff quarters would be available for the King and Queen with a specially reserved entrance and a heavily reinforced shelter in the basement. Although the Queen insisted that costs should be kept to a minimum, at the same time the decision was taken that the apartment should be considered as a fortress, hence blast walls, steel plates and shutters, bullet-proof glass, loopholes to bring fire to bear on the entrance passage and even a dedicated Tommy gun post were all added. Whilst no final details were given of how much it cost an

---

64 'Invasion Threat and the Reply', *The Times*, September 18, 1940
65 'Bombing of London Monuments', *The Times*, September 17, 1940
66 'German Contradictions – Divergent Statements on Raids and Invasion', *The Times*, September 16, 1940
67 Archibald Sinclair to Rt. Hon. Sir Alexander Hardinge, 20 June 1941, AIR20/5209, TNA
68 Eric de Normann to Sir Alexander Hardinge, 27 September 1941, WORKS19/1052, TNA

early estimate had been £12,500, a considerable sum of money and approximately £500,000 in modern terms. For protection the local Home Guard would be used along with military clerks working in the building but at times of 'emergency' up to a dozen troops would be made available.[69] By late February 1942 all of the alterations had been made and the accommodation was handed over to the Royal Household for its use but there is no evidence that any Royal visitors were ever received and in July 1945 it was handed back to the Ministry of Works.[70]

69 Ibid., E. de Normann to Lieutenant Colonel the Hon. Sir Piers Legh, 8 January 1942; de Normann to Legh, 28 January 1942
70 Ibid., de Normann to J.R. Wade, 20 February 1942

3

Protecting the King

Whilst preparations were being made for their safety the war went on and the King and Queen adapted to their new role. Albert, Duke of York, the second son of King George V and Queen Mary, had in 1923 married Elizabeth Bowes-Lyon, and in December 1936 following the abdication of his elder brother King Edward VIII, he had become his reluctant replacement and assumed the regnal name of King George VI.[1] Now three year laters, returning from Balmoral in late August 1939, the King – who was only 44 years old when Adolf Hitler's forces invaded Poland – and his wife quickly established a routine of spending the working day at Buckingham Palace and evenings and weekends at Windsor. Initially the Queen and her equerry Captain Sir Harold Campbell RN, "a charming, very helpful Naval officer", were transported daily to London in an enclosed Humber passenger armoured car which was described as "cramped and uncomfortable".[2] According to one source "the impression was given that they were permanently in London, and at times they flew the Royal Standard over the Palace when in fact they were not there" but it was only when the worst of the Blitz had subsided that they returned to London on a more permanent basis, visiting Windsor at weekends.[3]

Mindful of his wartime role and a veteran of the previous conflict, the King always appeared in uniform whenever in public having resolved that as long as the war continued he would not be seen wearing civilian clothes. Reflecting his own naval service for official duties this was often as an Admiral of the Fleet with its midnight blue material trimmed with gold braid which he wore when inspecting the bombing damage to the Palace. He also had his other service dress which he wore regularly and appropriate to the occasion.[4] He also eventually insisted that all male staff at Buckingham Palace and Windsor Castle were put into navy-blue battledress with the initials 'G.R. VI' embroidered on to the breast pocket. The Queen did not wear uniform, despite being head of the three

1   Denis Judd, *King George VI* (London; Michael Joseph, 1982), p.140
2   Mike Tompkin, 'A Reminiscence of 1940', January 1984 (Northamptonshire Archives), p.4; Brigadier Sir Jeffrey Darell, Bt, M.C., 'Memories of the Coats Mission (June 1940-January 1943)', n.d., Darell Papers (privately held). This account was almost certainly written in the summer of 1988 to be stored in the regimental archives and used by Julian Paget; Darell to Andy (?), 5 September 1988, 'Sir Jeffrey Lionel Darell Bt., MC, P/95569', D6, Coldstream Guards Regimental Archives (hereafter 'CGRA')
3   Vickers, *Elizabeth*, p.219
4   When at Windsor or Sandringham he did allow himself to wear grey flannels and a sports jacket; Corbitt, *My Twenty Years in Buckingham Palace*, p.156

women's services, and made efforts to maintain stylish outfits, although other female members of the wider Royal Family, such as the Princess Royal and the Duchesses of Gloucester and Kent, did wear their uniforms.[5] One biographer describes her wardrobe as being intended to emphasise "her position as a figure of peace" with gentle colours which were not too gloomy but also not too bright. With her brother Fergus having been killed at the Battle of Loos in 1915, there was no doubting her commitment to the fight against Hitler.[6]

Throughout that first autumn of the war and into the following winter and spring, the King made a number of official visits to inspect various Army contingents, air bases and naval stations. Every effort was made to keep his movements secret, indeed it had been stipulated in June 1938 that no reference was to be made to such visits other than retrospectively.[7] This did not always work, most notably in early September 1940 when the BBC reported his attendance at a service in Westminster Abbey shortly before it was due to take place but for the most part it did provide an element of security.[8] He had begun his visits within days of war being declared, touring "the GHQ of Britain's air defence" dressed in his Air Marshal's uniform with a side-cap and "gas mask slung over one shoulder".[9] His major visit to France in December 1939 to inspect the British Expeditionary Force and Royal Air Force was accompanied by a large party including the Duke of Gloucester. This was widely reported by the international media but the 2 January 1940 eighty-mile tour of various units based along the south coast of England, during which he was once again dressed in his Field Marshal's uniform, was only reported later.[10] That same month he made his first visit to Aldershot to meet with Canadian troops who were training there; for this initial inspction he was accompanied from Buckingham Palace by an escort made up of four men of the Royal Canadian Mounted Police. For a February 1940 trip, during which the King and Queen visited two air stations in the West Country, the press were reminded that there should be no report of their activities until the day following.[11] In April he reviewed the garrison at Dover Castle, the first visit by the monarch since George III when the country had last been threatened with invasion.[12]

5   Vickers, *Elizabeth*, p.219
6   Shawcross, *Queen Elizabeth*, p.496
7   Hardinge to Hankey, 2 June 1938, CAB21/2637, TNA
8   Ibid., 'Extract from the Minutes of a Meeting of the Civil Defence Committee held on 11 September 1940'
9   No title, *The Daily Mirror*, Thursday, 7 September 1939
10 'The Queen was in the parlour – the King was with his troops', *The Daily Mirror*, Tuesday, December 5, 1939; 'Army Notes', *RUSI Journal* (Vol.85, Issue 537; 1940), p.168; ibid., 'Air Notes', p.180; 'Army Notes' (Vol.85, Issue 538; 1940), p.364
11 Walter Monckton (Director General, Press and Censorship Bureau) to 'the Press', 5 February 1940, CAB21/2637, TNA; 'Air Notes', *RUSI Journal* (Vol.85, Issue 538; 1940), p.377
12 'Army Notes, *RUSI Journal* (Vol.85, Issue 539; 1940), p.585

On his visit to France on 6 December 1939 General Alan Brooke escorted the King as he inspected troops from the British II Corps.

General Maurice Gamelin, the French commander who the following summer would lead the failed attempt to defend his country, discussed the strategic situation with the British King.

The King takes the salute from men of the Oxford and Bucks Light Infantry
during one of his many visits to Aldershot.

He also inspected Allied troops such as Norwegian sailors who had
escaped to Britain to continue the fight.

As the war expanded and the British forces in France found themselves on the defensive the pace of his visits increased. In May and June along with the Queen he visited regiments in Dorsetshire and the West of England to confer decorations for gallantry to men who had been involved in the recent retreat to Dunkirk. In July he visited Aldershot twice more to inspect first the Australian contingent and then its New Zealand counterpart which were both supporting the defence of Britain. This followed two visits the month before to again inspect the Canadian troops still stationed there.[13] The last of these highlighted concerns that existed about the King's security and a fear that he was being deliberately targeted by the German *Luftwaffe*. A series of bombs had been dropped by enemy aircraft and although he was at least two miles away at the time the Ministry of Home Security wondered as to the possible motives as the area had not previously been attacked.[14] A discussion within the Joint Intelligence Sub-Committee concluded that it was "probably the long arm of coincidence" and asked, "if the Germans really wanted to bomb the King, would they have not sent more than two machines to do it and have dropped more than 15 bombs?".[15] The Monarch was not apparently deterred and he shortly afterwards undertook visits to the Royal Fusiliers training centre and the camps of the Scots, Welsh and Irish Guards where demonstrations were organised highlighting the training and equipment of the troops. In mid-August he was in West Wickham in Kent to watch 3000 men drawn from the Home Guard conduct various exercises with the official note registering that "the majority of the troops were fully armed and equipped, while the soldierly bearing and steadiness of all was especially noteworthy". A further visit to the Aldershot Command in early October included a demonstration of an anti-tank platoon who threw imitation Molotov cocktails at an 'enemy' tank whilst anti-tank rifles were fired at models. It was consequently decided not to include any reference to the incident in any of the daily summaries but offered further evidence of the anxieties that existed.

With all of these visits the King needed some form of physical security and following the move of the princesses to Windsor in late May 1940 the role to be played by the Metropolitan Police in protecting the Royal Family was modified. Throughout the inter-war period the King and Queen, the Prince of Wales, the Duke of York and the prime minister had all received "continuous and uninterrupted protection" from the police, added to which when attending public functions and at other unspecified times Special Branch officers were also provided.[16] For pre-war visits to Balmoral two of the latter based themselves near the local

13 Ibid., 'Army Notes' (Vol.85, Issue 540; 1940) pp.796-797; 'Army Notes', (Vol.85, Issue 539; 1940), p.585
14 Minute by Major O.G. Villiers (Ministry of Home Security), 7 July 1940, CAB21/2637, TNA
15 Ibid., C.T. Edwards to Major O.G. Villiers, 7 July 1940
16 Minute, 12 September 1926, MEPO3/557, TNA; ibid., 'Memorandum on Protection afforded by the Special Branch', 18 July 1929

railway station at Ballater "with the object of picking up any suspects who might travel North for the purpose of approaching or annoying Royalty".[17] The King's Detective, Chief Inspector Hugh Cameron, now requested that an additional police sergeant be employed to provide specific protection for the two princesses at Windsor.[18] The individual selected to guard the girls was Sergeant Kenneth Goodwill who had joined the police in 1932 and was attached to Rochester Row station. Only 28 years of age he had served as a protection officer to them and it was reported he had previously given "entire satisfaction and knows the Suite and servants".[19] This new arrangement did not last long, however, as the sergeant was withdrawn on 3 November and replaced by a constable from the local Berkshire Constabulary who was detailed with providing protection to them at Windsor. A plainclothes officer from the Travelling Staff was assigned for when they were travelling.[20] In July 1941 Cameron requested that an additional police constable be made available, making a total of nine men along with a police superintendent who would accompany the Royal Family and be available to provide "additional police protection to the castle during the hours of darkness".[21]

Cameron had an influential role to play in guarding the King and his family. Retiring as a Chief Superintendent in 1952, he had first been appointed as the then Duke of York's personal detective in 1930 after ten years of service, the previous four spent working as a sergeant in the clerical section of 'A' Division, or Whitehall Division, which was located in Westminster.[22] He was clearly very well regarded and just four years later, in October 1934, when an opening emerged he was put forward as "the best officer" to be the detective to Queen Mary. The Duke had initially asked that he be allowed to stay with him as he did "a great deal for him – much more than ordinary protection duty", but as the appointment carried with it a promotion it was agreed that Cameron should take up the opportunity and he was promoted to Sub-Divisional Inspector and transferred shortly afterwards.[23] Following King George V's death, in February 1936 Cameron returned to serve his youngest son and remained with him throughout the war.[24] A brief post-war newspaper description referred to a "tall, distinguished, and quietly well-dressed" man who did not really look like the popular conception of a "royal bodyguard,

17 Minute by Superintendent (Special Branch), 19 May 1952, MEPO38/150, TNA
18 Minute by Chief Inspector H. Cameron (Canon Row, 'A' Division), 22 May 1940, MEPO3/1893, TNA
19 Ibid., Minute by Superintendent David Storrier, 25 May 1940; 'Central Record of Service – Kenneth Mackay Goodwill', Metropolitan Police Heritage Centre, n.d.
20 Ibid., Minute by Cameron, 3 November 1940
21 Cameron to Storrier, 25 July 1941, MEPO38/150, TNA
22 'Return of officers who have been recommended for consideration of appointment as personal attendant on H.M. The Queen…', 31 October 1934, MEPO2/2382, TNA
23 Ibid., Minute by Commissioner, 6 November 1934; Brooke to Trenchard, 12 November 1934; Minute by ACA, 16 November 1934
24 Ibid., Confidential Memorandum by DACA, 8 February 1936

protector, and 'shadow'".[25] He had also, like George VI, served in the First World War, nearly five years in the Royal Horse Artillery and had joined 'A' Division as constable in the summer of 1919 shortly after he had been de-mobbed. It is also perhaps worth noting that he was born in Malvern in April 1894 and presumably knew the Worcestershire area well.[26]

At the same time the King was taking his own steps to safeguard his well-being. In June 1940 shooting ranges were laid down in the gardens of both Buckingham Palace and Windsor Castle where he and his equerries practised with a variety of small arms and he always carried a rifle in the car with him as well as a revolver.[27] The Queen also took instruction every morning in firing a revolver, reportedly using rats for target practise, and was equally resolute in her determination to fight against the invader.[28] During a visit to war factories in Coventry in August the King had been shown into a miniature range where he scored a bull's eye.[29] According to a story told to the American ambassador by Churchill's parliamentary private secretary and confidante Brendan Bracken, the Prime Minister had found the King practising with his rifle in the garden of the Palace and had been told by him that "if the Germans were coming, he was at least going to get his German".[30] On hearing this Churchill apparently said that he would get the King one of the only recently arrived Tommy Guns, which had been imported from the United States, "so he could kill a lot of Germans".[31] This episode pointed to the improvement that had taken place in the relationship between these two absolutely key figures who had not been close to begin but this improved rapidly as 1940 progressed. Both the King and Queen had been strong supporters of Neville Chamberlain and prior to the war's outbreak they had viewed its prospect with considerable apprehension.[32] A result of this was that George VI was no supporter of "the unreliable" Churchill, indeed he had been opposed to his inclusion in the Cabinet in September 1939 and, along with the rest of his immediate family, was suspicious about the prospect of his leading the country.[33] The memory of his support for his brother King Edward VIII during the Abdication crisis endured and in May 1940 the King was initially "bitterly opposed" to his appointment as the country's new prime minister. Throughout

25 'King's Bodyguard', *Glasgow Herald*, 2 February 1952, p.4; 'Central Record of Service – Hugh Joseph Ross Cameron', Metropolitan Police Heritage Centre, n.d.
26 'A Division – Inspector Hugh Joseph Ross Cameron', n.d., MEPO2/2832, TNA
27 Halifax Diary, 5 June 1940, cited in Bradford, *Reluctant King*, p.321; Lacey, *Majesty*, pp.138-139
28 Harold Nicolson (Nigel Nicolson, ed.), *Diaries and Letters: 1939-1945* (London; Collins, 1967), p.100; Sam Matthew, 'Queen Mother shot rats at Buckingham Palace to practise her aim in case of a raid by Nazi parachutists during Second World War', *Daily Mail Online*, 30 April 2015
29 'King and Queen in the Midlands', *The Manchester Guardian*, August 9, 1940
30 Joseph P. Kennedy, *Hostage to Fortune – The Letters of Joseph P. Kennedy* (New York; Penguin, 2002), p.457
31 Wheeler-Bennett, *King George VI*, p.463; Aronson, *The Royal Family at War*, p.29
32 Aronson, *The Royal Family at War*, pp.23-24
33 Ibid., p.25; Shawcross, *Queen Elizabeth*, p.507

the summer months the situation improved but Churchill acted for some time in the knowledge that even to his monarch he was not the first choice for the role.[34] Not until early September would the relationship appear to be restored fully as the two began a regular weekly Tuesday luncheon during which they served each other from a side table and talked freely with only the Queen present.[35]

The need to improve security surrounding the Royal Family became much more apparent as the capitals of Europe came under attack from the German military. In addition to the concerns about the potential bombing threat from the *Luftwaffe* during the summer of 1940, there were other grounds for concern. Peter Fleming was the first to reveal in his account of the invasion summer, published in 1957 that the use by the Germans of airborne forces whose purpose appeared to be to take hostage members of the European royal families had led to the recognition that there was "the need to provide the Sovereign with a personal bodyguard".[36] At the time concerns had indeed been expressed, Lord Hailsham, the former Lord Chancellor, had written to Churchill in mid-June 1940 highlighting his fears that the Germans would make the Royal Family a specific target.[37] As he observed, German forces had "made a desperate effort to capture the Royal family" in both Norway and Holland and he did not doubt they would do the same were they to attack Britain. No evidence has been found in the respective national archives to indicate that the Dutch, Norwegian or Danish authorities had made plans for evacuation of their senior royalty and, certainly in the case of the latter, this was to prove a serious oversight.[38] King Christian X of Denmark had been captured when his country was attacked on 9 April; his bodyguard, the Royal Life Guards, put up a brief fight but it was quickly apparent that there was little option other than to surrender. He chose to stay at home where his presence was warmly welcomed and he became a symbol of resistance to his people.[39] King Leopold of the Belgians, Commander-in-Chief of his country's military forces, also chose to stay with his people after he surrendered his armed forces in the face of the overwhelming German attack.[40] Despite a personal appeal from his British cousin, King George VI, he could not be persuaded to change his mind and the Belgian leader's actions would be judged critically in the years that followed.[41] And in Norway, German forces made at least two attempts to capture the government and royal family who fled on a special train from Oslo to Hamar, 80 miles inland. Both proved unsuccessful as did an air attack on the town of

34   Ibid., p.514
35   Bradford, *The Reluctant King*, pp.312-313, 339
36   Fleming, *Invasion 1940*, p.133
37   Hailsham to Churchill, 19 June 1940, PREM4/10/4, TNA
38   Correspondence with Netherlands Institute of Military History, 5 August 2010; National Archives of Norway, 22 November 2010; Statens Arkiver (Denmark), 30 July 2010
39   Trond Norén Isaksen, 'Danes at War', *Majesty: The Quality Royal Magazine* (Vol.36, No.4; April 2015), pp.20-24
40   Geoffrey Stewart, *Dunkirk and the Fall of France* (Barnsley; Pen and Sword, 2008), pp.93-94
41   Wheeler-Bennett, *King George VI*, pp.452-455; Bradford, *The Reluctant King*, pp.317-319

Elverum to which they had now moved although this destroyed its central district and killed a number of people. This was followed by another deliberate targeting of Nybersgund near the Swedish border as the Royal party sought safety.[42] After a total of two months of being pursued around his own country by the Germans King Haakon VII of Norway, or 'Uncle Charles' as he was known to his British relatives, was finally persuaded to reluctantly head to the west coast at Molde and leave his country on the evening of 7 June 1940 on the cruiser HMS *Devonshire*.[43]

The most conclusive evidence came with the attack on the Netherlands. The three airfields around the Dutch capital had been bombed early on 10 May 1940 after which attempts were made to land considerable numbers of airborne troops. Throughout the first day of the invasion the defenders at Valkenburg, Ockenburg and Ypenburg more or less managed to resist and hold on; the failure to capture these key strategic points would prove critical as it allowed the principal German targets to avoid capture. Queen Wilhelmina, the 59 year-old head of the Dutch people, was at the Noordeinde Palace and a plan was found in a downed aircraft which included detailed descriptions of how it could be reached; the Germans missed her by less than an hour. More than a week before the invasion of the Netherlands had begun Hitler had apparently given orders that Wilhelmina was to be captured. She would be "treated with military honours" if possible and allowed to live in one of her palaces in The Hague but under German guard; the alternative was to be brought to Germany as a prisoner.[44] Having insistd on staying, she was finally persuaded by the remaining Council of Minister members to leave the capital and set out from The Hague around 9pm on 12 May 1940 heading for Rotterdam.[45] From here she managed to escape to the Hook of Holland where she was taken aboard HMS *Hereward*; although she had initially hoped to be taken further south to join her troops the British vessel was forced to return to Harwich taking her as well. Upon arriving she telephoned King George VI in the hope of securing additional military support from him but the situation was hopeless and he persuaded her to proceed to London. He met her in person at

42 Bernard Ash, *Norway 1940* (London; Cassell, 1964), pp.82-84; Henrik O. Lunde, *Hitler's Pre-Emptive War – The Battle for Norway, 1940* (Newbury; Casemate, 2011), pp.226-230; Jack Greene and Alessandro Massignani, *Hitler Strikes North – The Nazi Invasion of Norway and Denmark, 9 April 1940* (London; Frontline Books, 2013), pp.131, 134-139; Halvdan Koht, *Norway – Neutral and Invaded* (London; Hutchinson and Co. Ltd., 1941), pp.76-89; J.L. Moulton, *The Norwegian Campaign of 1940 – A Study of Warfare in Three Dimensions* (London; Eyre and Spottiswoode, 1966), pp.96-99; François Kersaudy, *Norway 1940* (London; Arrow Books Limited, 1991), pp.78, 80, 110, 120

43 Bradford, *Elizabeth*, p.89; Shawcross, *Queen Elizabeth*, p.509; 'The Norwegian Campaign', *After the Battle* (Number 126; 2004), p.54; Kersaudy, *Norway 1940*, pp.171-174

44 Lieutenant Colonel E.H. Brongers, *The Battle for the Hague 1940* (Soesterberg; Aspekt, 2004), pp.31-36, 134-144; Walter B. Maas, *The Netherlands at War: 1940-1945* (London; Abelard-Schuman, 1970), p.33; Lord Strabolgi, *The Campaign in the Low Countries* (London; Hutchinson and Co. Ltd.; London, 1945), pp.46, 57

45 Herman Amersfoort and Piet Kamphuis (eds.), *May 1940 – The Battle for the Netherlands* (Leiden; Brill, 2010), pp.166-167; Cadbury, *Princes at War*, pp.131-133

Liverpool Street station and heard her stories of the German airborne attack and the attempts that had been made to seize her and her family.[46]

Hailsham's concerns appeared to have some basis and he also worried about what might happen if a German attack proved partly successful and captured the princesses warning that "it would be possible to bring tremendous pressure to bear on the King and Queen to accept intimidation by threatening death and even worse things".[47] Whilst his recommendation was that the two girls should be sent to Canada, what he almost certainly did not know was that at some stage following the invasion of the Low Countries and France, plans had begun to take shape as to how to tackle just this threat. There was a recognition that more needed to be done and an elite bodyguard was about to be formed with the sole, dedicated purpose of protecting the King and his family. The task appears to have fallen to the Hon. Piers Legh, a very senior member of the Royal Household who had wartime responsibilities which included both air raid precautions at Buckingham Palace and general oversight of measures for the monarch's protection. His background was similar to that of Hill Child, soon after the end of the First World War – during which he had served with the Grenadier Guards – he had been appointed as Equerry to the Duke of Windsor and remained with him until his abdication. Retaining the rank of Lieutenant Colonel but known to everybody as Joey Legh, he had then been appointed as Equerry to King George VI in March 1937 and four years later succeeded to the position of Master of the Household which he retained until 1954 when he retired having served three monarchs.[48] Sir Alan Lascelles who had worked alongside him described Legh in his obituary as "an admirable head of a department and an absolutely reliable organizer of any function that called for his supervision".[49] This seemed to be a particularly telling epitaph as, although there is no direct evidence, it can be reasonably assumed that he was instrumental in the establishment of the Coats Mission.

46 Wheeler-Bennett, *King George VI*, pp.450-451; Shawcross, *Queen Elizabeth*, p.508
47 Hailsham to Churchill, 19 June 1940, PREM4/10/4, TNA
48 'Obituary – Sir Piers Legh', *The Times*, October 17, 1955
49 A.L., 'Obituary – Sir Piers Legh', *The Times*, October 18, 1955

4

Coats' Mission

Even in the early months of the war manpower pressure was growing on the British Army which was required to strengthen its garrisons and forces not just at home but also in France and across the British Empire. This meant that compromises initially had to be made in terms of which forces were used to protect the Royal Family. At Windsor a company of Grenadier Guards had arrived within three days of the princesses being moved to the castle and a small number of the officers lived in and came to meals with them. These were from the Training Battalion where the Company Commanders were mostly veterans of the First World War who had been recalled "like tame elephants" to get the men into shape.[1] The sentries were issued with live ammunition and told to fire if anybody did not respond first time and obey a challenge from them. In addition there was a detachment of the Home Guard formed especially for the castle and headed by Owen Morshead, the librarian and archivist "whose perfect diction matched his tall and aristocratic appearance".[2] The group was a typical mix, those who were in reserved occupations, others who were medically unfit or waiting to be called up and veterans of the First World War; it was even rumoured that there were volunteers who had fought in the Boer War but kept their true age a secret.[3] Officially referred to as the Windsor Castle Defence Company they had a serious role with orders to counter any surprise enemy attack. If there were indications of an overwhelming invasion and no sign of any other defending forces they were to escort the Royal family to the airstrip at Smith's Lawn.[4] Presumably Wing Commander Edward 'Mouse' Fielden, who was at this stage Captain of The King's Flight, was to transport them away in the specially converted twin-engine Lockheed Hudson aircraft which carried two aircrew one who manned a machine gun at the front.[5]

---

1   Douglas Dodds-Parker, *Setting Europe Ablaze – Some Account of Ungentlemanly Warfare* (London: Springwood Books, 1983), p.29; Captain Nigel Nicolson and Patrick Forbes, *The Grenadier Guards in the War of 1939-1945 – Volume 1, The Campaigns in the North-West Europe* (Aldershot: Gale and Polden Limited, 1949), p.49
2   Shawcross, *Queen Elizabeth*, p.515; S.R. South, 'Recollections of the Home Guard in Windsor', The Royal Windsor Web Site – Histories of Windsor http://www.thamesweb.co.uk/windsor/windsorhistory/homeguard.html
3   Shawcross, *Queen Elizabeth*, p.527; Pimlott, *The Queen*, p.57; Ulick Alexander to E.H. Savill, 18 September 1940, CRES46/35, TNA
4   'Obituary: Capt Andrew Angus', *Daily Telegraph*, 17 November 2013
5   'Obituary – Wing Commander Tom Bussey', *Daily Telegraph*, 18 January 2010; 'Group Captain Edward Fielden' in Bernard O'Connor, *RAF Tempsford: Churchill's Most Secret Airfield* (Stroud: Amberley Publishing Limited, 2010)

The only known group photograph of the Coats Mission showing the assembled officers
from the Coldstream Guards and 12th Lancers with King George VI, Queen Elizabeth and
the two princesses. This was taken by P.M. Goodhead and Son, a well-known photography
business from Lynn, at some point during the Sandringham visit in January 1942.

One of Princess Elizabeth's cousins, who was staying at Windsor with her at this
time, was comforted by the idea of the bodyguard protecting the Royal family
until she "learned that although the operation probably included the corgis, it did
not include me".[6]

For Buckingham Palace and St James's Palace the decision was quickly taken
that it would be left to the various Holding Battalions connected to the Brigade
of Guards to mount the largely ceremonial King's Guard at both. In the case
of the Coldstream Guards, with the 1st and 2nd battalions both forming part
of the British Expeditionary Force, the primary purpose of its holding unit was
to provide a pool of reinforcements who could be posted overseas as required.[7]
It had been established in the early months of 1940 from the previous Training
Battalion and, during the more than three years it existed, its strength varied
between 900 and 3000 men formed into three companies. Having previously
formed up at Sandown Park it moved to Regent's Park Barracks in Albany Street
in central London, "a depressing place to live in, with its dingy barrack blocks,

6   Margaret Rhodes, *The Final Curtsey – A Royal Memoir by the Queen's Cousin* (Edinburgh; Birlinn
     Limited, 2012), p.68
7   Michael Howard and John Sparrow, *The Coldstream Guards 1920-1946* (London; Oxford
     University Press, 1951), pp.14, 17

long recognised as unfit for modern barracks and … its bleak and sandy square".[8] Here it remained until November 1943 when, as the re-named Westminster Garrison Battalion, it moved to Wellington Barracks which was much closer to the Palace. Professor Sir Michael Howard, who was one of the last members of the Holding Battalion and carried out ceremonial duties, described the role as "enormous fun" but confessed that "if there had suddenly been a parachute landing on [the palace], we wouldn't have had the faintest idea what to do, we would have called the police".[9] In addition to the Royal role these men took on various other duties. They were required to provide guards for the inner defences in Westminster which included 'dusk to dawn' patrols in Hyde Park. During the summer of 1940 groups also went out on a daily basis to prepare trenches in the northern suburbs of London where "they dug cheerfully and without misgiving". Between September 1940 and July 1943 there was also the guarding of the prime minister at Chequers – "the Special Area" – and some of the troops acted as wardens to Rudolf Hess once he was imprisoned in the Tower of London.

There was another role carried out by a small, select group of these men. Coldstreamers drawn from within the holding Battalion would also act as what George VI called "my private army" which was so secret that his official biographer provided few details and wrongly spelled its official title.[10] The German targeting of European royalty and the wish of the King and Queen to continue to carry out public engagements despite the knowledge of Hitler's plans meant that a bodyguard was vital and the initial leader of the eponymous mission was James, or more commonly Jimmy, Coats.[11] He had been born in April 1894 in New York City in the United States and educated at Downside School in Bath and Magdalen College Oxford.

His grandfather, also Sir James Coats, was the first baronet, a formal title which had been created on 5 December 1905 as 'Coats of Auchendrane, Ayrshire'. He had been born in Scotland in 1834 but 20 years later he had travelled to the United States and within three years he was married and living in New York City. Although he returned to Britain briefly, much of his life was spent in his adopted home country living in Providence, Rhode Island, where he was responsible for running the affairs of J. & P. Coats, his family's famous thread business which was a leading manufacturer of sewing cotton. Described as "diplomatic, tactful, and a trained executive" the contemporary references make it clear that his commercial skills were accomplished and the United States arm of the business was extremely successful. At the time he was made baronet the family company had become the

8   Ibid., p.17
9   Interview with Professor Sir Michael Howard, 15 March 2010
10   Fleming, *Invasion 1940*, p.133; Wheeler-Bennett, *King George VI*, pp.463-464; the mis-spelling resulted in both Aronson and Bradford repeating the same and it is only William Shawcross who has more recently corrected the error
11   'Memories of the Coats Mission', Darell Papers

third largest in the world by market capitalisation after US Steel and Standard Oil and it employed around 10,000 people in the thread mills where Coats had been born in Paisley back in Scotland.

In September 1914, shortly after the outbreak of the Great War, the younger Jim Coats was commissioned into the Coldstream Guards as a lieutenant and travelled to France.[12] During the war, and having been promoted captain, in December 1917 he married Lady Amy Gordon-Lennox, daughter of the eighth Duke of Richmond, and later a personal friend of the Duchess of York, the future wartime Queen Elizabeth.[13] He fought throughout the war seeing action at the battles of Passchendaele and Cambrai and was wounded and mentioned in despatches before, in January 1918, it was gazetted that Captain James Stuart Coats had been awarded the Military Cross.[14]

During the inter-war years he was a stockbroker but also had time to become an expert fisherman and shot. He is best known as having been a skeleton racer, indeed there was some suggestion that he was the finest ever tobogganer on the Cresta Run.[15] As one of his friends wrote in his obituary when referring to his sporting prowess, "this type of excitement was akin to his spirit of adventure; indeed any form of adventure was well within his compass".[16] Perhaps more significantly this period also saw

Jim Coats shown in 1941 with the Holding Battalion. Having inherited his father's baronetcy in 1959 he died seven years later at the age of 72.

---

12 One of his cousins, Lieutenant Archibald Coats, was killed in October 1918 whilst serving as an officer with Battery D, Nineteenth Field Artillery, American Expeditionary Forces; *History of the State of Rhode Island and Providence Plantations – Biographical* (New York; The American Historical Society Inc., 1920), pp.378-379

13 'Obituary – Lt-Col Sir James Coats', *The Times*, October 28, 1966

14 'Supplement to the London Gazette', 28 December 1917; Lieutenant-Colonel (temp) J. S. Coats, M.C. (42705); 'Sir James Stuart Coats Bt., M.C., P/42705', C15, CGRA; ibid., 'Notes for Obituary by Colonel Alex Wilkinson', 17 January 1967

15 From 1954 to 1956 he served as President of the St. Moritz Tobogganing Club. He had taken part in the 1948 Winter Olympics where at the age of 53 years and 297 days he came seventh in the skeleton luge making him the oldest ever competitor in this version of the games; 'Notes for Obituary by Colonel Alex Wilkinson', 17 January 1967, CGRA

16 Ibid.

him strengthen his connections with the Royal Family, for aside from his wife's friendship with the Queen, his brother's former wife was also one of her friends as was another of his sisters-in-law, Lady Doris Vyner. Indeed one of those who later served under him during the early stages of the Mission concluded that Coats was selected entirely because of his very senior friendships.[17] He was a known and trusted figure within the very senior Royal circles and this subsequently, almost certainly, gave him considerable autonomy to make key decisions when devising the plan for the family's future safety. Coats was described by one of the junior officers he commanded in 1940 as being "a successful businessman with great charm and full of energy and determination to get things done. With his experience, knowledge and connections he was an ideal choice for this appointment".[18] Another account refers to him as "a man of outstanding drive and determination" and he was "well suited to the task".[19]

His credentials for leading special missions were further endorsed in the war's first months when he was selected for another unique role which offered an opportunity for him to demonstrate his abilities. In addition to his other sporting interests he was also an excellent skier and his experience made him an obvious choice to command the Fifth (Supplementary Reserve) Battalion, Scots Guards, known more informally as 'the Ski Battalion' or 'The Snowballers'.[20] Established in early 1940 it was intended to join a French force, the *Chasseurs Alpins*, in providing assistance for the Finns who were then still resisting the December 1939 Russian invasion. This was a highly unusual body in that it included approximately 200 officers all who had volunteered to surrender their rank and be appointed as Guardsmen or NCOs; a total of 1000 men had volunteered although a large number of them had no experience of winter warfare. In addition there were 72 officer cadets and 200 others who had been enlisted from civilian life and included amongst them veterans of the Spanish Civil War and 'soldiers of fortune' including David Stirling and Michael Calvert who would both later become leaders in the establishment of dedicated special forces units.[21] The second in command was Major Bryan Mayfield from the Scots Guards who had spent the previous three years serving in Palestine. The unit moved to Chamonix in France at the beginning of March and trained using equipment that had been in store in Scotland since the end of the First World War, but with the Finnish position collapsing the British troops were recalled home and moved to Glasgow. They never made it any further

---

17 Interview with Darell, 18 August 2010; 'Notes for Obituary by Colonel Alex Wilkinson', 17 January 1967, CGRA. His father, who had become the second baronet in 1913, also served as a Conservative Member of Parliament representing the seat of Wimbledon and East Surrey
18 'Memories of the Coats Mission', Darell Papers
19 Peter Stewart-Richardson, 'Special Forces', in Julian Paget (ed.), *Second to None: The Coldstream Guards 1650-2000* (Yorkshire; Leo Cooper, 2000), p.154
20 Francis Mackay, *Overture to Overlord* (Barnsley; Pen and Sword, 2000), pp.38-45; David Erskine, *The Scots Guards, 1919-1955* (London; William Clowes and Sons Ltd., 1956), pp.21-26; 'War on Skis', *RUSI Journal* (Vol.85, Issue 537; 1940), pp.103-104
21 'Memories of the Coats Mission', Darell Papers

as the government in Helsinki surrendered. A senior figure in the Coats Mission later described the Ski Battalion as "absolute madness" and there is little evidence to suggest it would have had much in the way of a military impact, but it added to the stains of its commanding officer.[22]

Having relinquished his temporary promotion to Lieutenant Colonel, Coats returned to London and in mid-June he was posted, technically in to the Holding Battalion although his orders listed the actual posting as the regimental head-quarters, before he was selected for a new, even more, equally unusual mission.[23] The initial name given to the group of men under Coats' command was the 'Mobile Detachment' of the Coldstream Guards Holding Battalion and it was formally established on 3 July at the Duke of York's Headquarters at Regent's Park Barracks.[24] In addition to its commanding officer, Major Wilfred 'Gussie' Tatham, who had been a Master at Eton, and Lieutenant Wilfred 'Jim' Thompson were the two junior officers – sharing the same first name they seem to have been more commonly referred to by their middle names – along with seventy-five other ranks.[25] This included detachments from the Royal Signals, the Royal Army Service Corps, the Corps of Military Police and medical staff.[26] According to the regimental history, these three men had reported to GHQ Home Forces on 27 June 1940 where they were informed of their new duties before they departed immediately to conduct secret visits to three houses that had been selected as possible refuges.[27] This meant a road journey of more than 900 miles in Coats' large and expensive American car – a Graham Supercharger – to recce the prop-erties and the routes to be taken to them, all without being seen or talking with anybody.[28] Within two days, on 5 July the unit moved on to Elstree School where it grew rapidly to 120 Guardsmen with, in addition to Coats, Tatham as Company Commander and Thompson and another young lieutenant, Jeffrey Darell, taking charge of the two platoons.[29] During this time they would have prepared their initial plans for how the mission was to be conducted as the war went on around them. Several bombs were dropped on Elstree and nearby Boreham Wood but none of the men were injured although some of them helped dig out of the rubble of their houses those locals caught up in the Blitz.[30] It was also at the beginning of this period that the Coats Mission had its one recorded practice session at

22 Interview with Darell, 18 August 2010
23 Posting Notice, 20 June 1940, CGRA
24 Ibid., 'Sir James Stuart Coats Bt., M.C., P/42705'. The personnel file only shows him being appointed as commander on 9 October 1940 with its formal establishment
25 Howard and Sparrow, *The Coldstream Guards*, p.21
26 'Memories of the Coats Mission', Darell Papers
27 Howard and Sparrow, *The Coldstream Guards*, p.21
28 'Memories of the Coats Mission', Darell Papers
29 Freddy Day, 'The Coats Mission', n.d. (Privately produced manuscript written by one of the military police assigned to the Mission; kindly shared by Brigadier (Retd.) Peter Stewart-Richardson, September 2010)
30 'Memories of the Coats Mission', Darell Papers

Buckingham Palace when the King, apparently trying to impress his uncle King Haakon as to its merits arranged a demonstration. Unfortunately the men failed to appear when the alarm signal was issued and then "proceeded to thrash the undergrowth in the manner of beaters at a shoot rather than of men engaged in the pursuit of a dangerous enemy".[31]

The Commanding Officer of the bodyguard was apparently given no written orders but had been told that in an emergency he would escort the King and Queen to a place of safety, one of a number of country houses which had been earmarked for this role and had been preserved from requisition.[32] The Monarch and his wife were in theory supposed to keep one suitcase each packed and ready in the event of having to be spirited away.[33] Only the officers were aware of this plan, the guardsmen initially believed that they had been selected to act as guards and escort them to and from public engagements.[34] Coats was also told in person by General Sir John Dill, the Chief of the Imperial General Staff, that he could ask for whatever weapons, equipment or transport he considered necessary in order to carry out his mission. When he went to the War Office with his initial proposed establishment and list of equipment, he was told by a senior officer that nobody had ever been given permission to ask for anything they wanted; this individual was amongst the many who did not know about the Coats Mission and his reservations were clearly soon addressed. Perhaps in an attempt to avoid drawing subsequent attention to the Mission and its role, responsibility for making the necessary arrangements appears to have been given to a young adjutant who had only recently transferred into what was described as the 'General Staff Coordination' role.[35] This was a relatively minor branch of the General Staff based in the War Office in Whitehall but he reported directly to the Director of Staff Duties who was then Major General Archibald Nye; he had considerable influence and was later actively considered by Churchill as a possible Chief of the Imperial General Staff before eventually being given the deputy role.[36] The young General Staff officer later wrote that he "handled" the "small select force" whose job was "to get the Royal Family to Canada in the event of invasion" but he doubted if the King would have left.

Whilst there appeared to have been no formal orders there was, however, a set of printed instructions, titled 'Aide-memoire on the evacuation of the Royal Family in emergency', which was limited to a single page of directions and classified

---

31 Wheeler-Bennett, *George VI*, p.464
32 'Cuttings about the Coats Mission', n.d., Northamptonshire Yeomanry Papers, Northamptonshire Record Office, NY2/2; 'Memories of the Coats Mission', Darell Papers
33 Fleming, *Invasion 1940*, p.133
34 Stewart-Richardson, 'Special Forces', p.154
35 F.D. Goode, 'The War Office General Staff 1940 to 1942 – A Worm's Eye View', *RUSI Journal* (Vol.138, No.1; 1993), pp.31-33
36 Diary, 18 November 1941, in Alex Danchev and Daniel Todman (eds.), *War Diaries, 1939-1945: Field Marshal Lord Alanbrooke* (London; Weidenfeld and Nicolson, 2001), p.200

'Most Secret'.[37] Although not marked with the date it was issued, this document was signed by Brigadier John Swayne who was D.C.G.S. Home Forces from late June to October 1940 when he was promoted and moved to take command of 4th Division so it was produced during this period.[38] It confirmed that there had been plans made to evacuate the King and Queen from Buckingham Palace and the Princesses from Windsor but provided no further details beyond "possible destinations" which were referred to by code-words contained in sealed envelopes which have not survived. There was also no distribution list but confirmation that there were "recipients of copies of the plans concerned". The only named individual who had received a copy was Captain Bryan Adams RN who was the senior officer in the Cabinet War Rooms responsible for over-seeing its daily running and would have been expected to act as the relay for any messages to the Prime Minister. There was also confirmation that the order to move would be issued by GHQ Home Forces following a decision "almost certainly" taken by the War Cabinet acting on advice issued by Churchill's senior Army commanders. Although the military headquarters had by this stage moved to St Paul's School in Hammersmith, this decision-making process would most likely have taken place in the Cabinet War Rooms where, with the Blitz at its height, most of the key meetings were being held and, in the event of an actual invasion, it was assumed that its use would have become even greater.

Also included was a brief timeline to be given to the Chief of the General Staff, Home Forces, at this point Lieutenant General H.C. Loyd, who it would appear was expected to take the lead role in deploying the special unit. Upon receiving advice that the move of the Royal Family would shortly be necessary, and whether the War Cabinet had made a decision or not, he was to send the message 'Coats Mission Prepare' to Home Forces, HQ London Area, HQ Fighter Command and the Chief Commissioner of the Metropolitan Police notifying them all that the evacuation was imminent. This would place the Mission on 30 minutes notice to move. Once the formal decision had been made a second message would then be issued to the same recipients which was phrased 'X Coats Mission' where the X was the code for the house which had been selected to act as the refuge. In terms of providing advice to the King and Queen as to how this would work, there was also a second brief sheet detailing the anticipated procedure. If there was still a working Cabinet War Room a message would come from it intended for an un-named Equerry at Buckingham Palace and at Windsor for Major Sir Ulick Alexander or Commander Colles. If this was not possible military communications were to be used to contact Coats direct at Wellington Barracks to authorise him to commence operations with senior officers at Windsor also being contacted with a message titled 'Urgent Message to Privy Purse' which would be passed to

37 Brigadier J.G. Swayne, 'Aide-memoire on the evacuation of the Royal Family in emergency', n.d., WO199/293, TNA
38 'Obituary – Lieutenant-General Sir John Swayne', *The Times*, 18 December 1964

Ulick. The same would happen for the owners of the selected residence who were to receive the message 'Coats Arriving'. This instruction appears to have remained unchanged until April 1941 when a minor hand-written amendment specified that there were now only two sealed envelopes containing the codes, the one held by Adams and the other by Loyd.

Although it had been assembled for some months, the unit was only officially established on 9 October 1940 by which point its size had increased to 140 men with a third platoon having been added led by Lieutenant Ian Liddell.[39] It had a unit call sign for its vehicles, a white 101 on a red background, and they all carried a blue light at the front which helped ensure that "the convoys were probably the fastest and safest in the country".[40] On 15 November the men moved once again from Elstree School to new billets at 'Bushey Golf Club'.[41] There were actually two golf courses in the area and the evidence would suggest that the Coldstreamers of the Coats Mission were in fact based at Bushey Hall near Watford. This was a mansion built in 1865 which had been turned into a high class country hotel and golf course at the turn of the century but had been requisitioned during the First World War and used by the Guards as a training depot. Once more a hotel at the start of the Second World War, it would have been known to the Mission's principals and it was also ideally situated as the North Western Avenue bordered the golf course and this would allow the troops to more rapidly leave London and head for the chosen country house. The key piece of evidence to support this being the headquarters is that the house that was used by the commanding officer was located in the road opposite the entrance. It also unusually had no listed official role until it was requisitioned in late 1942 when the site was taken over by the United States Army Air Forces Eighth Air Force Fighter Command. This coincided with the beginning of the Mission's disbandment.

When it was established, the platoons each contained 33 men, with a junior officer in the lead supported by a senior NCO, three corporals and 28 privates split into a small headquarters and three sections.[42] With 24 men in the Company Headquarters and another 17 in the Mission Headquarters, this was the unit's full strength, effectively nine infantry sections. To transport this force initially there were four 32-seater civilian Leyland single-decker coaches with drivers from the Royal Armoured Service Corps who provided 12 men under Sergeant Pritchard. In addition there were two three-ton and another two 15cwt trucks to carry the unit's equipment, a staff car for Coats and an ambulance. The men were

---

39 'Coats Mission – War Establishment', 9 October 1940, M.E. Hancock Papers, Documents.826, 1988-02, Imperial War Museum (hereafter 'IWM'); Howard and Sparrow, *The Coldstream Guards*, p.21; Darell to author, 25 November 2010

40 Day, 'The Coats Mission'; Stewart-Richardson, 'Special Forces', p.154

41 Howard and Sparrow, *The Coldstream Guards*, p.22

42 Day, 'The Coats Mission'; 'Protection of the Royal Family in War', Commander J.R. Stephens RN, 2 April 1965, WO32/21796, TNA; these notes were used for reference when considering the role of the post-war equivalent

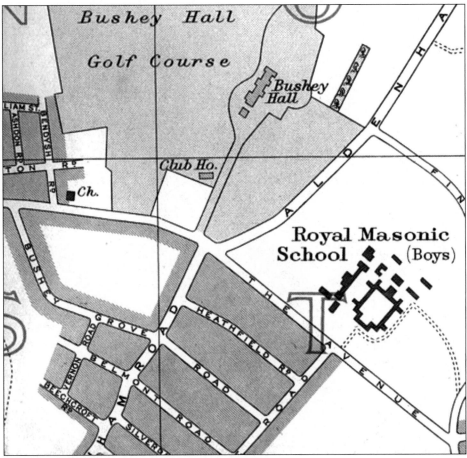

A map from 1939 showing Bushey Hall and also Belmont Road; No.30 was used by the successive commanders of the Coats Mission as their headquarters.

initially lightly armed carrying mostly rifles although there were a small number of light machine-guns, two anti-tank rifles and three two-inch mortars. Although there was ammunition in reserve carried in the trucks, the troops for the most part carried 50 rounds each. By the summer of 1941 there were now 14 vehicles available to move the troops with the primary form of transport still being the 32-seater coaches. At the same time its firepower had increased greatly. According to one of the officers, "the one thing that we had to do was to be able to up sticks at any moment, take up the defence of whatever house had been chosen and the Mission would be absolutely armed to the teeth of course, and fully capable of going to any part of the country as required".[43] Whilst he and his fellow officers

43 Interview with Hancock, 1984, IWM

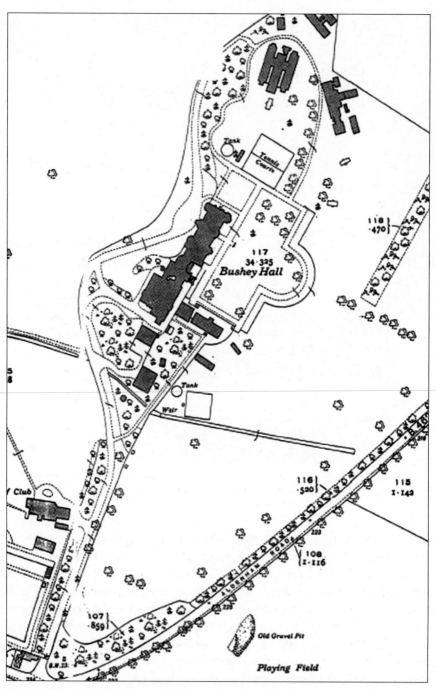

A larger detailed map of Bushey Hall from 1940 showing the grounds and the buildings. This mansion dated from 1865 and had been requisitioned during the First World War to be used by the Guards as a training depot. The Coats Mission arrived there in November of that year and remained until the unit was disbanded in January 1943.

(L-R) Lieutenant Wilfred 'Jim' Thompson, Captain Malcolm Hancock, Major Wilfred 'Gussie' Tatham, Captain Tim Morris, Lieutenant Michael Humble-Crofts, Lieutenant The Hon Julian Holland-Hibbert, Lieutenant Ian Liddell.

carried just their pistols and the majority of the men were armed with rifles, there were also now a dozen light machine guns, 14 Thompson submachine guns, two anti-tank rifles, 232 grenades and three two-inch mortars along with more than 400 rounds of explosives or smoke. The unit had 65,000 rounds of ammunition, two-thirds of which was kept in reserve, but even so its fighting power was still more likely limited to a light, mobile role which would be incapable of fighting off anything more than an infantry attack. How it would have fared against an airborne attack supported by Stuka dive-bombers and Messerschmitt fighters, the standard German approach to such operations, is not clear although presumably this was the possibility for which it trained.

Aside from its main role the Mission was initially given the additional task of reinforcing the troops guarding HQ Fighter Command at Bentley Priory, about four miles from its headquarters, if it was attacked by parachutists. This extended to dealing with any Germans who might have landed in Elstree and covered an area extending to the Edgware Road.[44] Tactical exercises were conducted with local troops – specifically the 30th Guards Brigade under Brigadier Alan Adair, which included 4th Battalion Coldstream Guards, GHQ Reconnaissance Unit, as well as units of the Irish Guards and Household Cavalry, and various Home Guard units – until July 1941 when they were relieved of this unpopular additional commitment.[45] This welcome move came about as result of a direct intervention by the King who was worried that it might impact on the mens' ability to carry out the special instruction.[46] The arrangements were made although Lieutenant-General Sir Bertram Sergison-Brooke, the commander of London District, made it clear that he was unhappy to be losing highly trained troops from his defence plan and suggested that "the King would be well advised to remain 'put' in Windsor Castle".[47] The Coldstreamers were also liable to be called

44 Howard and Sparrow, *The Coldstream Guards*, p.21; Lieutenant-General H.C. Loyd (CGS, Home Forces) to Lieutenant-General Sir B.N. Sergison-Brooke (HQ, London District), 6 May 1941, WO199/293, TNA
45 Howard and Sparrow, *The Coldstream Guards*, pp.22, 298
46 Major Sir Ulick Alexander to Brigadier C.G. Nicholson, 3 May 1941, WO199/293, TNA
47 Ibid., Sergison-Brooke to Loyd, 10 May 1941

out for evening practice without any warning.[48] On a few of these occasions the callouts were actually genuine due to reported sightings of parachutists who had been 'seen' in the searchlights during bombing raids but were later recognised to have been anti-aircraft shells bursting in the light.

Inevitably in such a small unit the officers were key to its functioning effectively and this included promoting a tight cohesion amongst the men. According to one of them it was "a very special body of men with whom it was a great pleasure to serve. We had a unique and historic role that dated back to the original role of the Household Division – the personal protection of The Sovereign".[49] The Guardsmen who were chosen in the summer of 1940 had to have exemplary conduct sheets and were interviewed personally by Coats to ensure they were suitable for the highly secret mission.[50] The regiment's official history refers to this being a period for those involved which lacked "excitement, because they were never, fortunately, called upon to fulfil the role for which they were brought into existence".[51] Another of the younger junior officers described it as a self-contained attachment without any of the normal duties associated with regular battalions, it was "the story of a happy family and a posting to it was much sought after".[52] As one of the older officers made a point of explaining when he was interviewed some years after the war, there was "tremendous competition amongst the guardsmen to get into the Coats Mission".[53]

Although it was named after him, it was not Coats but perhaps Tatham who was key as the original commanding officer reportedly did not actually have a great deal to do with the Mission and his company commander "really ran it all".[54] He was a great athlete with a very good physique; born in December 1898 in Bromley, Kent, in 1924 he was a AAA Champion in the 440 yards hurdles, the same event at which Harold Abrahams secured two awards before later going on to win the gold medal in the 100 yards at the Paris Olympics. This achievement came four years after he been part of an Oxford and Cambridge team that secured a world record time during a 4 x 880 yards relay race in Philadelphia, and he also ran in the semi-finals of the 1928 summer Olympics.[55] Before that he had joined up in August 1917 and was awarded a Military Cross three days before the armistice "for conspicuous gallantry and devotion to duty" during an action fought near La Longueville when he was attached to the 1st Battalion, Coldstream Guards. In the inter-war period despite being a Master at Eton Tatham retained his regi-

48 Day, 'The Coats Mission'; Howard and Sparrow, *The Coldstream Guards*, p.22
49 'Memories of the Coats Mission', Darell Papers
50 'Obituary – Brigadier Sir Jeffrey Darell, Bt', *The Times*, 15 March 2013
51 Howard and Sparrow, *The Coldstream Guards*, p.22
52 'Memories of the Coats Mission', Darell Papers; Howard and Sparrow, *The Coldstream Guards*, p.22
53 Interview with Malcolm Hancock, Catalogue Number 7396, 1984, Reels 11, 12, IWM
54 Interview with Darell, 18 August 2010
55 'Memories of the Coats Mission', Darell Papers; 'Wilfred George Tatham OBE M.C., P/21893', T6, CGRA

mental connection and in February 1934 he had been appointed as a captain in the reserves. This meant he was amongst the first to be called up for service in August 1939, despite fierce opposition from his Head Master who wanted to him to remain at the school, and eventually posted to the Coats Mission the following summer.[56] In many respects a professional soldier with considerable experience of how the wider regiment worked, one of his colleagues remembered him to have been very efficient and that he "gave tremendous thought to all these arrangements which we had to make" although he had absolutely no sense of humour.[57] Coats took over command of the Holding Battalion of the Coldstream Guards on 11 February 1941, where he remained until it was disbanded at the end of 1943 apparently regretting that he had never had the "chance of meeting the Germans in battle again"; he was succeeded by Tatham who, appointed as a Temporary Major, retained command for a further 13 months.[58]

Thompson was the senior platoon leader, known to all as 'Bloody Jim', "a very big farmer" who lived in King's Lynn near the Sandringham Estate before an emergency commission in March 1940 led him to join the regiment. Born in Lincolnshire in February 1912, in addition to being a good rugby player and a pace bowler who played cricket for Norfolk and the M.C.C, he was also a scratch golfer who partnered the King in a foursome at Hunstanton Golf Club during the Christmas 1941/1942 visit to Sandringham.[59] He had been one of three subalterns selected for an earlier "special job" and was sent on 31 May 1940 to Dunkirk to assist with the evacuation where he remained before returning across the Channel three days later; his posting date to the Coats Mission was also listed as 17 June 1940, the same as his new commanding officer.[60] When he finally left the Mission nearly two years later on 9 August 1942 he was the last original member who had been present at the initial meeting at GHQ Home

56 Ibid., Tatham to Colonel (?), 28 February 1940
57 Interview with Hancock, 1984, IWM
58 Howard and Sparrow, *The Coldstream Guards*, pp.17, 23; 'Sir James Stuart Coats Bt., M.C., P/42705', CGRA; ibid., 'Notes for Obituary by Colonel Alex Wilkinson', 17 January 1967. Coats retired in September 1945 with the honorary rank of Lieutenant Colonel and a third Mention in Despatches. He returned to the Stock Exchange, Whites Club and winter sports before, in July 1959, he succeeded his father and was created 3rd Baronet Coats. When he died in October 1966 his estate was valued at £78,232, more than £1.3 million in current terms. As for Tatham, when the Coats Mission disbanded, he was seconded to the 2nd Battalion Hampshire Regiment which was short of officers and deployed to North Africa. He was captured in December 1942 following the Battle of Tebourba and Mentioned in Despatches. Moved to Italy, he appears to have escaped following the armistice in September 1943 but was re-captured a month later and spent the remainder of the war as a POW. He was for a time the British Council representative in Yugoslavia and was awarded an OBE in 1954 before retiring to St. Helena where he died in August 1977; 'Wilfred George Tatham OBE M.C., P/21893', T6, CGRA; ibid. Rachel Tatham to Colonel Trew, December 1943
59 'Memories of the Coats Mission', Darell Papers; Interview with Hancock, 1984, IWM; 'Wilfred Sydenham Thompson, P/124545', T7, CGRA
60 Ibid., Major W.T. Towers-Clark to Lieutenant Mitchell, 15 April 1944

Temporary Captain
Liddell pictured
in Europe during
the advance into
Germany.

Major Ian Tubbs was the final
commander of the Coats Mission.
Despite having taken this high-
profile role he was not selected for
a subsequent command and the
suggestion was that he was not thought
the most capable leader of men.

Forces and the longest serving officer.[61] Transferring with him back at the beginning was Darell, or Jeff as he was more commonly known, who was just 20 years old when he was posted to join Coats. He had been commissioned into the Coldstream Guards in July 1939 as a second lieutenant and was later evacuated with 1st Battalion from the beaches at La Panne although it is not clear if he met Thompson during the chaotic final days in France.[62] On 1 June he was at Tisbury in Wiltshire with his unit when the call came that he was being transferred. He reported to his commanding officer, Colonel Arnold Cazenove, who was held in great regard amongst Coldstreamers, and told to report to London immediately. There he met with Colonel Guy Edwards who told him that he was to take over a platoon in a new organisation commanded by Jimmy Coats who had an office at Wellington Barracks and was waiting to see him. On reporting there his new role was explained to him along with the composition of the Coats Mission.[63] When Tatham eventually took charge Darell became Company Commander before himself leaving to return to 1st Battalion, Coldstream Guards that same summer. He would go on to have a long and distinguished military career later taking part in the Normandy landings and winning a Military Cross in March 1945 during the fighting in Germany.[64]

The final one of the junior officers who made up the initial cohort, Liddell, was also only 20 years old when he had been commissioned into the Coldstream Guards on 2 November 1940 having initially enlisted at the war's outbreak as a private in the King's Shropshire Light Infantry.[65] He had been born in Shanghai in October 1920, his father being the chairman of a family merchant trading firm based in China. Although he was the last to arrive – once again the posting notice appears later than the date he arrived, his acting lieutenant posting dating from 11 February 1941 – he was appointed to lead Number 2 Platoon. Remembered for his musical talent, during the winter 1941 visit he had been responsible for producing 'Cinderella', the annual Christmas pantomime performed at

61 Howard and Sparrow, *The Coldstream Guards*, p.22. He was released from service in October 1945 with the rank of Temporary Major and returned to Norfolk where he died in December 1988; 'Wilfred Sydenham Thompson, P/124545', T7, CGRA
62 'Memories of the Coats Mission', Darell Papers; 'Sir Jeffrey Lionel Darell Bt., MC, P/95569', CGRA
63 Ibid.
64 Ibid. He was commanding 5th Battalion Coldstream Guards as a Temporary Major when he led an attack along the main Xanteen-Rheinberg road, 'Obituary – Brigadier Sir Jeffrey Darell, 8th Bt', *The Daily Telegraph*, 29 March 2013; 'Obituary – Brigadier Sir Jeffrey Darell, Bt', *The Times*, 15 March 2013. Remaining in the army, from 1947 to 1948 he attended the Staff College at Camberley and in 1961 he was appointed Commandant at Sandhurst. The most successful of the officers who served in the Coats Mission, he did not retire until September 1974 with a final rank of brigadier and his last military role as the Queen's A.D.C. before later serving as High Sheriff of Norfolk and enjoying a long retirement only dying in 2013
65 'Ian Oswald Liddell VC, P/156048', L7, CGRA. One of his Housemasters at Harrow, writing a reference for Liddell's application to join the Coldstream Guards, felt he could not offer an unreserved recommendation "because of a certain lack of force in his character"; L. Gorse to Captain L.G.C. Neame, 27 June 1940

Sandringham, which was subtitled 'So What! and the Severn Twirps'.[66] The Royal Family attended a performance given at the Village Hall in West Newton in January 1942 and joined in when 'Old Macdonald had a farm' was sung "with the appropriate snorts and noises"; Princess Margaret was apparently fascinated by the song and "practised afterwards until she rendered it perfectly", something about which the King joked with him a few days later. Promoted to captain in February of the following year, he landed in France shortly after D-Day as part of the Guards Armoured Division. He died just 18 days before V.E. Day; a month later it was confirmed that he had been awarded a posthumous Victoria Cross for his role in the capture of a critical bridge over the River Ems.[67] This proved to be the final such award during the war against Germany involving anybody from the British armed forces.[68]

Other than the expansion that took place during its early months, the Mission's size remained largely the same. By December 1941 there were 144 men with five officers, six warrant officers and sergeants along with 16 attached drivers and mechanics from the Royal Army Service Corps.[69] The recorded strength for March 1942 still listed five officers with Major Ian Tubbs having recently arrived to take command. Born on 1 January 1902, he was another Eton man and a professional soldier who has joined the regiment as a second lieutenant in 1922 and was serving as Company Commander in 1st Battalion, Coldstream Guards when the war broke out, as part of the British Expeditionary Force.[70] He was, however, removed from the position in February 1940 as the conclusion was reached that he was not "tactically efficient" and he spent the next two years filling various positions in the Holding and Training Battalions before this appointment to the Coats Mission.[71] His Company Commander was Captain Malcolm Hancock who had been with the Mission since May 1941 and was another of the older officers who had been called up at 43 years of age and given an emergency wartime commission. During the Great War he had served with the Northamptonshire Regiment and was later seconded to the West African Regiment and, in the space of five weeks in the summer of 1916, he was awarded a Military Cross and Mentioned in Despatches.[72] His real profession was "starting

66 'Memories of the Coats Mission', Darell Papers. Max Hastings in an article on Liddell's life describes his Coats Mission role as "a socially delicate but militarily unpromising role"; Max Hastings, 'Cold, calculated bravery', *The Spectator*, 16 April 2005
67 'Ian Oswald Liddell VC', in Lance-Sergeant L. Pearce, *A Short History of the Regiment's Victoria Cross Holders* (Regiment Headquarters; September 1988), pp.27-28; Clare Bristow, 'His bravest solo', *Classic Magazine (Sunday Express)*, April 30, 1995; Steve Snelling, 'Suicidal Valour', *Britain at War Magazine*, March 2013, pp.106-113
68 Peter Ryde to Major Louch, 10 May 1993, 'Ian Oswald Liddell VC, P/156048', CGRA
69 'Coats Mission – War Establishment', 24 December 1941, WO199/298, TNA
70 'Ian Noel McClymont Tubbs, P/17(?)', T6, CGRA. he retired as a Major in 1947 and died in May 1974 at his home near Cheltenham
71 Ibid., Tim (?) to Lieutenant Colonel Harcourt-Vernon, 23 October 1943
72 'Malcolm Ernest Hancock M.C., P/136997', H12, CGRA

race horses" and his obituary published following his death in 1989 focussed on his long service with the Jockey Club allowing only a single sentence to his time spent with the bodyguard.[73] He had subsequently left in June 1942 before being posted to a role with GHQ Home Forces working with the Auxiliary Forces, the specially selected Home Guard troops who had been assigned an insurgent role in the event of a German invasion. Supporting the more senior officers, Thompson and Liddell continued to lead platoons along with the Hon. Lieutenant Julian Holland-Hibbert.[74] Later termed the 5th Viscount Knutsford, the latter had joined the Mission in June 1941 and was another of those who would go on to subsequently fight in North Africa where he was badly wounded and invalided out of the military.[75] The 'GHQ Operation Instruction, Special No.A' dated 31 July 1942 showed that Tubbs still remained in command with the now promoted Captain Thompson as his deputy and Lieutenants Faller, Liddell and Holland-Hibbert commanding the three platoons.[76] Having been posted as an Acting Lieutenant earlier that month, John Faller, known as Ben on the account of his middle name 'Benson', was the final officer to be posted to the Coats Mission. Born in Buenos Aires in September 1921 where his father was the chairman of the local Harrods branch, he remained with it until its disbandment the following year and was later also seriously wounded during the Battle of Monte Cassino.[77]

Despite the frequent changes in leadership throughout 1941 the Coats Mission developed a strong sense of readiness and cohesion as it trained constantly to prepare for its principal role. In March of the following year, however, an order was issued from HQ London District, under whose authority it operated, that a quarter of the men should change every three months. With the recent fall of Singapore and the loss of tens of thousands of British and Imperial troops in the Far East the manpower position was becoming acute. This change allowed troops to be transferred out of the 'garrison' role of guarding the Royal Family to provide reinforcements for fighting units. This process was repeated in June and November and was a "cause of much regret, for the continuity of personnel had been well preserved, among guardsmen as well as officers, since the Mission's earliest days". With the transfer of troops and replacements arriving frequently, the role of training exercises became of added importance in order to keep the changing body of troops ready for any potential action. By the spring of 1941 onwards the Coldstreamers had been undertaking these for several months preparing for "very strenuous, very mobile operations", an experience described as being "a lot of training and hard work".[78] This formed the staple for the men

73 Interview with Darell; 'Obituary – Lieutenant Colonel M.E. Hancock', *The Times*, 9 May 1989
74 Howard and Sparrow, *The Coldstream Guards*, p.22
75 Interview with Hancock, 1984, IWM
76 'GHQ Operation Instruction, Special No.A', 31 July 1942, WO199/292, TNA
77 'John Benson Faller, P/219051', F3, CGRA. His injuries led to his being invalided out of the regiment but he survived to live a long life dying in 2010 following a stroke
78 Ibid.

and the exercises appeared designed to toughen up stamina and improve marksmanship. In early July 1942 Number 1 Platoon conducted a march, presumably involving their supporting vehicles, from Whitchurch to Cirencester where they then carried out a series of exercises with the local Home Guard detachments before being brought home by train from Kemble.[79] During late July and August the entire body of men carried out training on the firing ranges at Singleton in Sussex, and in September another of the platoons conducted a training march from Bushey to Cambridge carrying out exercises with the Home Guard at each of their overnight stops along the way.[80] Plans were also made to update the transport available, with it being proposed by the commanding officer that one coach and one heavy lorry should be replaced by four smaller lorries which would improve the unit's mobility, but it is not clear if this was accepted.[81]

There was in fact a growing decline in official interest in the Coats Mission as the threat of a German invasion of Britain receded to the point where it was thought increasingly unlikely to happen. It was perhaps not a surprise therefore when in December 1942 it was confirmed that the King had agreed to the proposals put to him that the Mission should be stood down "for the time being". The now increasingly acute issue for the senior officers responsible for its organisation were the manpower pressures beginning to threaten the Brigade of Guards. From the debacle of France up until June 1942 there had only been two battalions committed to the fighting, but from this point the Coldstream Guards suffered considerable losses in the Middle East and were struggling to find replacements.[82] It was also increasingly believed that any move by the Germans to once again develop an invasion capability would provide a long warning period for the defending force to be stood up once more; such was the success of Allied intelligence and the information provided by Ultra decrypts that any move to conduct even a raid would almost certainly have been detected in advance. It was therefore proposed that when the Royal Family travelled to any of its homes outside of London arrangements would be made for their protection "to be undertaken by troops specially detailed for the purpose". Most parts of the country had significant numbers of troops on hand for most eventualities as British and Canadian units were joined by large numbers of Americans that were beginning to arrive in preparation for the anticipated assault on occupied Europe. The Coats Mission went to Sandringham for the last time during the first fortnight of October 1942 and at the end of the tour the officers were invited to bring their wives to a cocktail reception where Princess Margaret sang 'Old Macdonald' once again.[83]

79 'Training of GHQ Units', 1 July 1942, WO199/298, TNA
80 Ibid., 'Coats Mission – location of', 25 July 1942; 'Training of GHQ Units', 17 August 1942; 'Training', 14 August 1942
81 Ibid., 'Transport – Coats Mission', 7 May 1942
82 Ibid., GHQ to Legh, 9 December 1942
83 'Memories of the Coats Mission', Darell Papers

The process of dismantling the unit was to be completed by 9 January 1943 although its basic structure, including equipment and buildings that had been requisitioned for its use, were to be retained in case it was needed to be re-established. It was assumed that if this happened the Brigade of Guards would provide these troops and HQ London District still remained in charge overall with the instruction that they would receive a fortnight's notice from GHQ if the order was to be rescinded. The only element that was re-assigned was the light ambulance and medical orderlies who were transferred to the supporting mobile force, the Morris Detachment, for its sole use.[84] On 2 January 1943 the rear party of the Coats Mission left Bushey for Regent's Park Barracks and was officially disbanded a few days later.[85] There was another unexpected final duty for some of the men when the King visited North Africa in June 1943 and stopped at the Villa Germaine in Algiers. Perimeter security was assigned to the Coldstream Guards, several of whom had been in the Mission and were recognised by the King.[86]

In April 1943 a further significant overhaul was conducted during which it was determined that HQ London District would be given a fortnight to establish any possible successor and this remained the case until 16 November 1944 when the final disbandment notice was given.[87] At the same time the general operational instruction was issued which confirmed that alternatives residences had been identified in Northern and Western Commands, the choice of which would "be recommended by C-in-C Home Forces to the War Cabinet in the light of the situation at the time".[88] Still operating from Bushey the proposed strength had been reduced to two officers, three junior officers and approximately 120 other ranks. In the event of an emergency arising the message 'Coats Mission Prepare' was to be sent to all those involved, including Major Sir Ulick Alexander as well as the Commissioner of the Metropolitan Police and the owner of the selected house. The troops were to travel with three days rations, their defence stores and spare fuel for 300 miles which was in addition to a similar amount carried by the mobile detachment. Upon arrival the message 'Coats Mission Present' was to be sent and communications were to be established with the nearest military commander who would also make available a mobile column of at least one company to provide reinforcements. The duties of the guard were also detailed with the first being listed as "to protect the King and Queen".[89] They were to stop any unauthorised persons not carrying a special pass issued by a Royal Equerry

---

84   Minute from Major General Philip Gregson-Ellis, 14 December 1942, WO199/298, TNA; ibid., 'Coats Mission – War Establishment', 18 December 1944; 'Disbandment – Coats Mission', 23 December 1942
85   'Memories of the Coats Mission', Darell Papers
86   Day, 'The Coats Mission'
87   Minute by CGS Home Forces, 3 April 1942, WO199/292, TNA
88   Ibid., 'GHQ Operation Instruction, Special No.A', 3 April 1943
89   Ibid., 'Duties of the Guard', Appendix B

from entering the perimeter. The only exceptions were staff from the chosen residence who would have their own specially issued passes and anybody who had been vouched for by the police. Military vehicles were to be kept under cover and defence works concealed. None of these details had changed from the instruction issued the previous year.

Accommodation that had been reserved for the Mission's use within the London area, should it have been reformed, was only finally released in November 1944; this included the innocuous property in a row of residential housing in Bushey which had been used by successive commanding officers from Coats through to Tubbs.[90] This decision was taken because of the Chiefs of Staff Appreciation produced in October 1944 which finally ruled out the possibility that Germany might attempt either an air or seaborne invasion other than "the possible exception of an attempt by a small force of parachute troops to carry out some spectacular coup".[91] Despite the latter perhaps appearing to have a particular direct relevance to such high value targets as the King and Queen, as a result the decision was taken that the houses and the dedicated force that was to protect them were no longer needed.[92] The following month arrangements that had been put in place for the emergency movement of King Haakon and Queen Mary were also finally cancelled an action which marked the formal ending of the Coats Mission.[93]

Even with this decision and the suspension of the dedicated role played by the Coldstreamers, the Mission did not in fact come to end. They had always only been part of the plan that was hastily developed in the summer of 1940 and given the catch-all title of the Coats Mission. Almost immediately it had been formed it was determined that the purpose of assembling an elite force of Guardsmen was that they might move in advance of the Royal Family to the emergency residence to which they were being evacuated and make the preparations to provide all necessary protection for their important guests. This is why Coats and his men were based in the northern suburbs of London allowing them to leave the city as quickly as possible west or north. The much more telling, and indeed potentially vital, role was actually played by another unit that formed the more visible bodyguard within the King's Private Army.

90 'Accommodation – Coats Mission', 21 November 1944, WO199/298, TNA. The property was 30 Belmont Road, one of a pre-war constructed row of houses
91 Colonel F.C. Drew to Major Sir Ulick Alexander, 24 October 1944, WO199/293, TNA
92 Ibid., 6 November 1944
93 Ibid., 'Subject – Move of Royalty in emergency', 12 January 1945

5

The Morris Detachment

In addition to the infantry there were also to be troops of armoured cars whose role was to transport the Royal Family in the event of an emergency.[1] They would not just provide the escort but also, and absolutely critically, remove the King, Queen and two Princesses from wherever they happened to be when the order to move them was given. This potentially meant they would have to fight their way into an area under intense attack and fight their way back out again, and, at least initially, this was likely to be a desperate battle. In terms of even the area around Whitehall and Buckingham Palace even by the late summer of 1940 the defending forces were still only limited. As a result of a review conducted in May, which had sought to create a contingency plan not only for an invasion but also a raid by up to 500 enemy troops, the fixed defences had been strengthened; following this there were still less than 1000 soldiers and Home Guard available should an attack take place, the majority of whom were Grenadiers at Wellington Barracks.[2] Further anti-aircraft defences were recommended in September once the Blitz had begun but, had there been an attack, the King and Queen's daily London residence would almost certainly have been the scene of fierce battles involving a stretched defending force.[3]

Whilst this might have been thought a natural role for the Household Cavalry, who traditionally acted as the escort, it was simply not in a position to carry out this role during the early wartime years. Men from it had spent the end of August and September 1939 filling sandbags for Windsor Castle and their own Combermere Barracks which, when formed into walls, were treated with cement wash.[4] Meanwhile the King's Life Guard, which from 1932 was based at Hyde Park Barracks, turned out on foot and in service dress khaki on 1 September and when it did offer a mounted guard its members were moved back and forth by furniture vans and old buses.[5] With a composite Household Cavalry regiment being shipped to Palestine in February 1940, as part of the first and only British cavalry division

---

1   Major W.A. Morris, 'The Morris Detachment', *The XII Royal Lancers Journal* (New Series, No.1; June 1946), p.20
2   Mike Osborne, *20th Century Defences in Britain: The London Area* (Market Deeping; Concrete Publications, 2006), p.32
3   'Defence of Whitehall', WP(40) 383, 24 September 1940, CAB66/12/13, TNA
4   'The Household Cavalry Regiment', in *The Household Brigade Magazine* (London; Gale and Polden Ltd., Spring 1940), p.40
5   Brian Harwood, *Chivalry and Command: 500 Years of Horse Guards* (Oxford; Osprey Publishing, 2006), pp.121-122

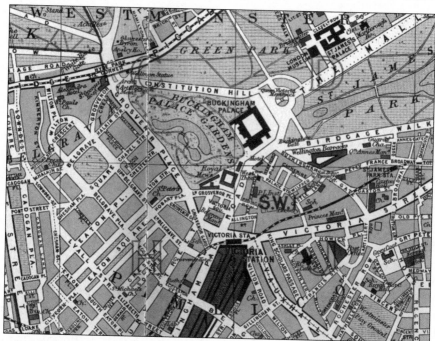

Map from 1939 showing Buckingham Palace and the adjacent Wellington Barracks where the Morris Detachment was initially based during its first summer.

An example of the Guy Mark I armoured vehicle which were being used by 2nd Northamptonshire Yeomanry. A total of 50 of these were produced and they were the first British armoured car with an all-welded construction. Above the centre of the hull was mounted a turret with two machine guns with the engine located at the rear. Adapted before it was used by the two princesses, these were cramped vehicles in which to travel.

of the war, reservists were left behind to staff the Training Regiment and organise and maintain defensive positions around London. Hyde Park was secured using barbed wire wrapped around the Household Cavalry's riding school jumps. After the invasion of the Netherlands more specific operational tasks were given to the approximately 350 men available to the Training Regiment.[6] Despite only having six automatic weapons and a small amount of other equipment they took responsibility for the defensive position known as the 'Acton Line' and were driven to their positions using civilian buses but only on week days during union hours as the civilian drivers went home in the evenings and on weekends. To repel any German advance towards London they also had 60 elderly horses which had been ruled unfit for front-line service, a furniture van and an old motorbike.[7]

With no spare capacity or equipment, it was for this reason that the mobile duties of the Coats Mission were given to 12th Royal Lancers. On Saturday 29 June 1940 a signal had been received at the regimental headquarters in Poole in Dorset where they were then re-forming.[8] They had led the advance into Belgium the month before and then been amongst those who escaped from Dunkirk complete only with their Bren guns and anti-tank rifles which they had stripped from their armoured cars before having to leave the vehicles behind. The signal gave orders for a senior subaltern or captain and nine other ranks, who were Rolls-Royce armoured car drivers and machine gunners, to be sent to London "for escort duties". The actual party was larger than had been asked for, eleven men led by Lieutenant Tim Morris, and by the following evening they had arrived at Kneller Hall in Hounslow. Only weeks before Morris, then the Regimental Signals Officer, had narrowly avoided capture in the small French town of Doullens.[9] As he reported to the headquarters for Home Forces situated at St Paul's School his men – four troopers and four Lance Corporals overseen by Lance Sergeant John Thurston – received their replacement armoured vehicles which they were to use for their as yet unrevealed new role.[10] This young officer wrote in October 1941 to Field Marshal William Birdwood, the regimental Colonel-in-Chief, with his own account of what had happened during these hectic days.[11] He confirmed to the distinguished retired officer, previously Commander of the Australian and New Zealand Army Corps during the Gallipoli Campaign and a Commander-in-Chief, India, that at the end of June 1940, when the regiment was at Poole, his commanding officer, Lieutenant Colonel Geoffrey

---

6   Orde, *Second Household Cavalry Regiment*, pp.4-5
7   Paget, *The Story of the Guards*, pp.191-192; Russell Braddon, *All The Queen's Men – The Household Cavalry and the Brigade of Guards* (London; Hamish Hamilton, 1977), p.193; Colonel The Hon. Humphrey Wyndham M.C., *The Household Cavalry at War: First Cavalry Regiment* (Aldershot; Gale and Polden Ltd., 1952), pp.5-9
8   Morris Detachment Diary, June 1940, 12th Lancers Archives, Derby Museum and Art Gallery, 912L: 2088/45 (hereafter 'DMAG')
9   'Record of Service of the Regiment during the War – France 1939-40', *The XII Royal Lancers Journal* (New Series, No.2; December 1946), pp.10-11
10 Morris Detachment Diary, July 1940, 12th Lancers Archives, 912L: 2088/45, DMAG
11 Ibid., Major Tim Morris to Field Marshal Birdwood, 24 October 1941, 912L: 2089/34

A metal plate, used presumably as a sign for their office at Windsor, showing Morris as the detachment's commanding officer and Humble-Crofts as his deputy.

Clifton-Brown, had been asked to find ten men to take up an escort role involving armoured cars in London. Morris was selected as the officer and allowed to choose the nine best men in the regiment. This small group received their orders direct from GHQ Home Forces and had been told that they were "to act as a mobile protection to the Royal Family should invasion occur".

By the end of the first week of July the detachment, which was initially referred to as the 'Morris Mission', had reported to the Holding Battalion Grenadier Guards at Wellington Barracks adjacent to Buckingham Palace. The Lancers were in fact issued with elderly vehicles, two very ancient Rolls-Royce armoured cars of 1920 vintage and a Lanchester which had been in the Regiment many years before. Within a week they also had received four of the Guy Armoured Car Mark I while the Lanchester was sent to the Mill Hill Workshops in north-west London to be converted into a passenger carrying vehicle. It was "very old and in poor mechanical state" but with the guns and fittings removed two comfortable seats were installed and despite it being "far from ideal and totally inadequate in every way for carrying the Royal Family in case of an emergency" there was nothing else available at that point.[12] Despite its refurbishment the Lancers were

12 Morris, 'The Morris Detachment', p.20

nonetheless "disgusted with this monstrosity" that had already seen several years of service in the desert and was mechanically below standard.[13] The men spent the next three months in London making refinements to the vehicles available to them. Now completely re-equipped, they also began training with the new equipment taking the vehicles to the ranges at Farnborough to fire the BESA guns. This was followed in August with a number of visits to Kent and Suffolk which were also recorded in the unit's diary.[14] When it was not training, the detachment was confined to barracks throughout the summer the only other activity being exercise in St James's Park across the road. Despite the secrecy involved with their role they were able to expand from the initial complement and find additional men and the transport needed to carry petrol and rations. In the middle of the month Morris was promoted to Temporary Captain and along with the newly promoted Sergeant Thurston, also recently confirmed as having won the Military Medal during the campaign in France, and one of the troopers, he visited the Humber works to view the new armoured staff car that was being prepared for transporting the King and Queen.

At least for the first few months a troop of supporting armoured cars was also provided from 2nd Northamptonshire Yeomanry which, during the summer of 1940, had become part of the 20th Armoured Brigade within the 1st Armoured Division. In a register produced in September this entire brigade only had a total of 64 vehicles and the vast majority of them, also the Guy Armoured Car Mark I, were with the yeomanry unit. It had been formed in May 1939 and was located around the county until the expanded German offensive which led, the following May, to the men and their vehicles moving to Dalham Hall, Newmarket in Suffolk where they were organised in a light armoured role as part of what was termed the Yeomanry Armoured Detachment.[15] At the end of June they moved to a new site near Guildford and shortly after their arrival two junior officers were summoned late one evening by their commanding officer, Lieutenant Colonel Otho 'Minnow' Prior-Palmer, and told, "I haven't the foggiest idea what this is all about but I've been ordered to send a troop of four armoured cars up to London tonight and I am sending you".[16] This was because with no other similar specially protected passenger vehicles available the troop had been selected to join the Coats Mission.[17] The two young officers, Lieutenants Michael Humble-Crofts and Mike Tompkin, departed as quickly as they could taking with them their vehicles plus a van which had been requisitioned and still had its 'Air France'

13 Day, 'The Coats Mission'
14 Morris to Birdwood, 24 October 1941, 12th Lancers Archives, 912L: 2089/34, DMAG; ibid., Morris Detachment Diary, August 1940, 912L: 2088/45
15 The 1st and 2nd Northamptonshire Yeomanry 1939-1946 (Uckfield; Naval and Military Press, 2014), pp.107-108
16 Tompkin, 'A Reminiscence of 1940', January 1984, p.2
17 'Return of Tanks in the Hands of the troops in the UK on 29 September 1940', Appendix 13, DC(S)(40)70, CAB70/2, TNA

Queen Elizabeth exiting one of the 'Special Ironside Saloons' most likely on 13 November 1940 when she used the vehicle to visit the Ex-Servicemen's Association on the Brompton Road.

livery on the side. The following morning they reported at St Paul's School where they met Coats and Morris but, at this stage, neither could tell him why they were there. It was not until a couple of days later that a briefing explained the role of the Mission and the part that would be played by the supporting armoured vehicles.

With the Lancers based at Wellington Barracks and given responsibility for transporting the King and Queen, the troop provided by the Northamptonshire Yeomanry was assigned to Windsor where it was to protect the two Princesses. As Tompkin later wrote, with invasion seeming probable and almost the entire equipment of the British Army having been left in France and the Low Countries, he was "the lucky possessor so to speak of four of the very few armoured cars in the country – available for either fighting or passenger duties".[18] Two cars were also sent to the Royal Army Ordnance Corps workshops at Mill Hill for conversion and had their guns removed along with the rigid "spine-jarring" seats and in their place were installed two small armchairs for Princess Elizabeth and

18 Tompkin, 'A Reminiscence of 1940', January 1984, p.3

Morris standing alongside one of the Humber 'Special Ironside Saloon' vehicles, very possibly in Wellington Barracks. This gives a good idea of its size particularly in terms of the height. M.1303563 was the first of the vehicles to be delivered and was collected from GHQ Home Forces on 13 September 1940. The car was driven by Trooper Rosling who had become the regular vehicle driver with Morris also travelling in the vehicle.

Princess Margaret which, once the possibility of evacuation was at an end, were later removed and the previous seats restored.[19] They also had floor matting added and attempts were generally made to make them more suitable for the duties now assigned to them.

Following the completion of the work the troop moved down to Windsor with the men and vehicles accommodated in the mews and the two officers being quartered with the 2nd Household Cavalry Regiment at Combermere Barracks.[20] Before they arrived Tompkin had joined the recce group which had been sent to examine the houses which might be used for evacuation visiting Worcestershire, Shropshire and Yorkshire to review the routes that would need to be taken to reach them.[21] Back at Windsor the troop began to practice and prepare for its role, a large part of which seemed to consist of driving at night. One of the cars was inspected by the King and Queen, and Tompkin also took the two princesses

19 Ken Tout, 'Royal evacuation; Letters to the Editor', *The Daily Telegraph*, 5 April 2013
20 'Memories of the Coats Mission', Darell Papers
21 Ibid.; Tompkin, 'A Reminiscence of 1940', p.3

along with their governess and a corgi on a trial trip around the Home Park.[22] Elizabeth and Margaret apparently enjoyed taking part in exercises in which they were able to sit in their specially converted vehicle driven by Sergeant Paul Curtis with Darell as outrider in his car.[23] The order of march for the Windsor troop were it to move to one of the houses in the summer of 1940 had Tompkin in the lead armoured car. He was followed by the second vehicle, one of the hastily converted armoured cars, carrying the princesses and their governess with the other carrying the detective and Equerry followed by a lorry carrying food and petrol and the rear armoured car with Humble-Crofts.[24]

The beginning of the Blitz led to a change in mid-September with the King and Queen spending more of their time at Windsor which meant that the Lancers were transferred there and moved into Combermere Barracks.[25] With the move of the Lancers it was also decided that the Northants Yeomanry were no longer needed but Morris requested an additional officer and arranged for Humble-Crofts, who he knew wished to transfer into the regiment, to join him along with ten of the troopers.[26, 27] With these changes move and the increased threat to the Royal Family both from the air and a possible invasion, it was decided that in addition to the armoured fighting vehicles there should also be some kind of bullet-proof saloon cars which the King and Queen could use during their visits to London and in case of air raids.[28]

The first Humber armoured saloon was delivered to the Lancers on 13 September with a second five days later.[29] With a body built by the coachbuilders Thrupp and Maberly and the armour manufactured by the Sheffield-based Spear and Jackson, they were known as 'Special Ironside Saloons'.[30] A total of six were made, a derivation of the Humber Light Armoured Car, sometimes referred to as 'Light Reconnaissance Car'. Manufactured by the Rootes Group these had been rushed into service in June 1940 following the losses of equipment suffered during the evacuation from France and by 1943 more than 3600 had been built. The special version manufactured for VIP passengers included a relatively luxurious interior and a split Perspex screen to separate driver and passengers. A side door was also provided to make entrance and exit easier although this compromised

22 'Memories of the Coats Mission', Darell Papers
23 'Royal evacuation…', *The Daily Telegraph*, 5 April 2013
24 'Memories of the Coats Mission', Darell Papers
25 Morris Detachment Diary, September 1940, 12th Lancers Archives, 912L: 2088/45, DMAG
26 Day, 'The Coats Mission'
27 'Memories of the Coats Mission', Darell Papers; 'Obituary – Lieutenant-Colonel Michael Tomkin' (sic), *Eastern Daily Press*, 5 August 2008. Tompkin was eventually posted to 5th Royal Inniskilling Dragoon Guards in February 1941 and, post-war, he would eventually be appointed as High Sheriff of Suffolk.
28 Morris to Birdwood, 24 October 1941, 12th Lancers Archives, 912L: 2089/34, DMAG
29 Richard Doherty, *Humber Light Reconnaissance Car 1941-45* (Oxford; Osprey Publishing, 2011), pp.11-13; B.T. White, *Tanks and Other AFVs of the Blitzkrieg Era, 1939-1941* (London; Macmillan, 1972)
30 G.F. Howard (Director) to Ministry of Home Security, 31 July 1944, WO199/297, TNA

the integrity of the armour which otherwise "offered good all-round protection against small-arms fire and limited protection against bomb splinters". Two more were delivered in December both of which had small bullet-proof windows. The left-hand front seat back squab could be folded forward and the Perspex division panel moved to the right to facilitate access to the rear seat. Equipment in the rear compartment included a clock, a microphone to communicate with the driver, and a fire extinguisher. There was a woollen rug and hide upholstery on the seats while the lower panels were covered with West of England cloth. This new car was used for the first time on 10 October when the King and Queen were driven from Buckingham Palace to Windsor by Trooper Rosling with Morris also in the car and the trip was repeated later in the month.[31] They looked like civilian cars and even had ordinary number plates and were pressed into use for the almost daily runs from Windsor to central London. When the refitted Lanchester finally returned it was still deemed to be unsuitable for special duties and was never actually used.[32] From January 1941 onwards the Special Ironsides were gradually replaced by Pullman Limousines. These had special bullet-proof austenitic steel coachwork but because of the extra weight there were initial problems with tyre blowouts until Dunlop supplied some heavy duty versions.[33] They were described as being comfortable to ride in but were very small and difficult to get in and out of although this apparently did not deter the Queen from using them.

Making the King and Queen's daily journey even quicker was the group of 'Red Caps' who were permanently attached for traffic duties. Led by Sergeant Bill Hazlewood, initially there were ten men although two more were later added and all were expert mechanics and motor-cycle riders.[34] This unit had famous origins, Sir Malcolm Campbell had been asked during the late spring of 1939 to form a Territorial motorcycle unit within the Corps of Military Police, which was intended to work in close cooperation with the mechanised London Division. Dubbed the 'Bluebirds' their role was to provide "a highly efficient traffic control system" and, once it had been stood up at Regent's Park Barracks that April, it had a strength of just over 100 men divided into a headquarters section and six other sections of 16 men. Referred to as 1st London Territorial Division Provost Company, each of its sections operated under the control of a sergeant and two corporals with the remainder of the men all lance-corporals. There were 15 motorcycles and one heavy truck which carried equipment allowing them to be fully mobile ranging from road sign equipment to cooking apparatus. Each man was armed with a pistol and on each machine there was a long burning lamp which would allow them to illuminate signboards at night. Known to his men as 'the Captain' or 'Sir', Campbell deliberately recruited men who had excelled

31 Morris Detachment Diary, October 1940, 12th Lancers Archives, 912L: 2088/45, DMAG
32 'Memories of the Coats Mission', Darell Papers
33 Day, 'The Coats Mission', p.3
34 Morris Detachment Diary, July 1940, 12th Lancers Archives

A list showing the available motorcycles in January 1941 being used by the military police outriders.

MOTOR CYCLES		
NORTON	W.D. NO.	4381738
NORTON	W.D. NO	4381739
NORTON	W.D. NO.	4386318
NORTON	W.D. NO.	4386338
NORTON.	W.D. NO.	4334486
NORTON	W.D. NO.	4334484
NORTON	W.D. NO.	4334488
NORTON	W.D. NO.	4334489
NORTON	W.D. NO.	4334490
RUDGE. 4.	W.D. NO.	4328564
RUDGE. S.	W.D. NO.	4328566
ARIEL.	W.D. NO.	4313659
VELOCETTE.	W.D. NO.	4328668

ATTACHED PERSONNEL	
CORPS OF MILITARY POLICE.	
y684578	Sergeant. W. Hazlewood.
y684420	Corporal. W. Tait.
y684595	L/Corporal. T. Austin.
y684019	L/Corporal. A. Chapman.
y686682	L/Corporal. F. Day.
y684594	L/Corporal. K. Fisher
y686644	L/Corporal. W. Giddy
y684584	L/Corporal. L. Rosoman
y684403	L/Corporal. N. Richards
y686683	L/Corporal. P. Whitehead.

The ten men from the Corps of Military Police serving with the Morris Detachment in January 1941; Freddy Day's name can be seen amongst them.

in motorsport and the company included many professional racing riders; they had to be proficient not just in the riding but also in mechanical skills needed to keep their bikes going and it was intended that each section would act with a considerable degree of autonomy.[35] The "Bluebirds" had trained at Burley Camp in Hampshire where they learnt how to conduct their core duties, signposting roads, despatch riding, point-duty work, directing transport and even more conventional police duties. As it was also intended that these men might provide support to a unit if it were shorthanded in emergency, they also received training with most of the weapons then available in the regular Army.[36]

Freddy Day was one of four men who were initially selected for service with the military police detail.[37] He later remembered that he had been called into his Commanding Officer's room and interviewed by "two gentlemen from the War Office". At the end of this he was told to report to a Major Coats of the Coldstream Guards at Wellington Barracks and drove up from near Dover to London arriving in the early morning. A meeting with Coats followed in a room overlooking Birdcage Walk when the men were told that they would be forming part of the bodyguard for the Royal Family. The leader of the Coats Mission also gave them Local Purchase Orders so they could go out and replace their Army issue vehicles with "a decent motorcycle that would do the job". Eventually they would be issued with Norton Model 18s, powerful 500cc machines, and when these wore out and there were no more spares available they were given American 'Indian' machines, although these were much less effective on cross-country terrain. They would ride ahead of the guardsmen and when the vehicles came to a crossroads or major junction they would stop all the traffic allowing them to proceed at maximum speed. As one of the officers in the Mission put it, "time would have been absolutely vital and they did a marvellous job in that way".[38] Indeed the "Bluebirds" proved "invaluable at getting the detachment through the most congested parts of London at high speed, as well as being used on many occasions as special dispatch riders for carrying important messages on long distances".[39]

Once the various elements were fully assembled the unit was then reorganised in November 1940 with an expanded establishment, the promotion of a number of the junior NCOs and a new name, the 'Morris Detachment'. This allowed for the process of planning and training which had begun back in June to be

35 Captain Sir Malcolm Campbell, 'The Corps of Military Police', CMP/RMP Historical Facts and Information, Third Quarter 1994; Major S.F. Crozier, *The History of the Corps of Royal Military Police* (Aldershot; Gale and Polden Ltd., 1951), pp.37-46
36 Alec Menhinick, 'With Territorial Motorcyclists in Camp: "Jolly Good Company"', *Motor Cycling*, August 23, 1939
37 Day, 'The Coats Mission', p.2
38 Interview with Hancock, 1984, IWM; Darell, 'Memories of the Coats Mission'
39 Morris, 'The Morris Detachment', p.22

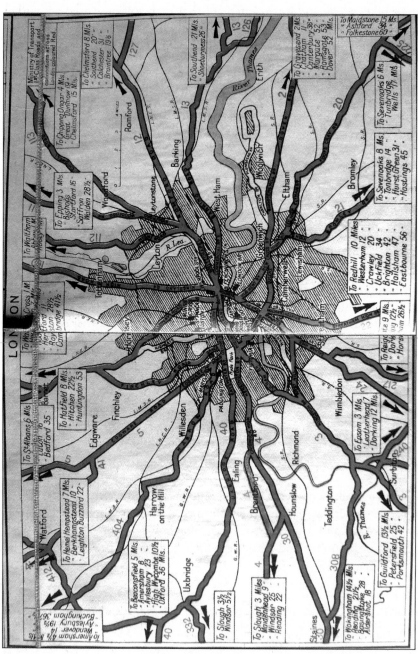

A large scale road map of central London from 1940 showing the key 4 and 40 routes both of which could have been used by the Morris Detachment to move the Royal Family to Windsor and then on to their selected refuge. For the Coldstreamers based near Watford they were also well placed to head west or north depending on which of the houses had been selected.

A group photograph of the Morris Detachment with Morris and Humble-Crofts seated centrally on the front row surrounded by their NCOs (the insignia on his lower arms suggests that it may be Sergeant John Thurston sitting to the left of Morris). The name of the unit's dog is not known.

increased in tempo with the veteran Lancers taking the lead.[40] According to one of the Coldstreamers, the role of the mobile detachment was to "make their way as fast, as quickly as they could, we would make our way and we'd hope to get up their together".[41] The decision was therefore taken to concentrate on developing a very fast moving column as speed was deemed to be essential although it was recognised that safety was also of paramount importance. Lots of training runs were made with the motorcyclists ranging up and down the column but with one of them always out at the front with the lead armoured car. His role was to travel in advance and signal if the road ahead was clear or not. In order to do this effectively the motorcyclists had also trained as drivers of the larger vehicles to hekp them understand how visibility on these was much reduced and this helped strengthen the relationship between the two elements of the convoy. It was also felt that the best chance of security came with keeping the Royal car moving at all times and during those daily runs that were made from Windsor in to London along the A4 an average speed of about 50mph was kept irrespective of the weather or road conditions as the motorcycle riders stopped the traffic ahead of them. In March 1941 it was proposed to split the column into two convoys when travelling, and that it would be accompanied by three police cars which would allow the same men who protected the King in London to be used at all times even

40 Day, 'The Coats Mission', p.4
41 Interview with Hancock, 1984, IWM

(L-R) Parked in front of Windsor Castle, a Pullman Limousine, a Humber 'Special Ironside Saloon' and one of the wheeled armoured vehicles, most likely the Daimler Mark II Scout Cars which arrived in 1942.

With the castle in the background, this was the first of the bullet-proof Pullman Limousines to be delivered to the Coats Mission. It had the civilian plate M.226514 and was collected personally by Morris on 10 January 1941 from Slough.

when travelling.[42] Throughout this period, a lot of practice was also given to night driving and immediate reaction drills in the event of an emergency, pointing to a belief that the evacuation would take place under cover of darkness.[43]

The men were effectively always on standby and leave was restricted with only one third of them being allowed out at a time. Prior to going out they had to give exact details of where they would be and at what times so they could be contacted if there was an emergency; the duty member of the military police along with the standby truck driver could then go and find them and bring them back. At Windsor they were restricted to being no more than 20 minutes away from the castle and this time included not just returning to camp but also getting ready to move off.[44] At Balmoral there was very little to do, a liberty truck would take the men into Ballater picking them up no later than 10pm.[45] The near constant practice and the restrictions imposed upon the men did, however, result in a highly trained group and a column which was able to cover considerable distances in a short period of time.

Training expanded to incorporate greater challenges for Morris and his detachment, along with the Coldstreamers, for the most part designed by Gussie Tatham who "was very good at writing imaginative and interesting exercises".[46] Sometimes these were held against other armoured units but these also involved infantry, usually one of the regiments from the Guards Brigade. Two other groups were often used for these "Sunday schemes" playing the role of the enemy, one being the Eton Officer Training Corps, "very enthusiastic" young gentlemen who "appeared to enjoy physical contact with their enemy", and the other the American Home Guard also known as the 'Red Eagles'. Organised by Charles Sweeney, who had finished the previous war as a colonel and now acted as Adjutant, and commanded by Brigadier Wade Hayes, a peace-time investment banker who had fought in 1898 Spanish American War, they had been established in July 1940 as an unofficial group. About 70 men in total, the formal unit owed its existence to a special order that had been issued by the King making these volunteers eligible for membership of the Home Guard. There was considerable hostility to the idea from Joseph Kennedy, the American ambassador in London. Hayes, who had gone on to serve on General John Pershing's staff during the First World War, refused to be cowed by Kennedy despite his even threatening to have his American citizenship revoked.[47] The unit consisted mainly of American businessmen who lived and worked in and around London – described as being mostly "paunchy, grey-haired, and affluent" – with professions ranging from investment banking

42   Alexander to Gregson-Ellis, 6 March 1942, WO199/297, TNA
43   'Memories of the Coats Mission', Darell Papers; Stewart-Richardson, 'Special Forces', p.154
44   Day, 'The Coats Mission', p.7
45   Ibid., p.14
46   'Memories of the Coats Mission', Darell Papers
47   Lynne Olson, *Citizens of London: The Americans Who Stood with Britain in its Darkest, Finest Hour* (New York; Random House, 2010), p.128

to the law, architecture and a number working in the film industry.[48] They were probably the best equipped Home Guard unit in the whole of Britain "with a lethal armoury of [Thompson] machine guns, [Winchester] automatic rifles and pistols" not to mention eighteen camouflaged armoured cars all of American design.[49] They also offered excellent hospitality in the headquarters, "somewhere near the A40", where after training runs the men would return for a drink and cigarettes and their hosts "were most generous in producing luxuries" that had not been seen for some time.[50]

Despite the equipment they had, the first exercises conducted with the Americans reminded one of those involved of his childhood "playing cowboys and Indians", and they were known more widely as "the gangsters" in part because of their Tommy guns but also because of their refusal to play by the rules. Over a period of time, and following training by Guards instructors, their fighting qualities became much improved and these initially "quite hilarious afternoons" later provided some real value for the men of the Mission as they tested themselves against a well-equipped and motivated opponent. In fact it was the American Home Guard who were involved in what was perhaps the most infamous training exercise conducted by the men of the Coats Mission. The 'Red Eagles' had been given the role of assisting with the protection of Lieutenant General Sir Bertram Sergison-Brooke, commanding London District, in the event of an invasion.[51] They were escorting him to a Sunday lunch in Ascot with Lady Portarlington and the Mission was tasked with capturing the general who appears to have been unaware of the potential for some disruption to his journey. The plan involved a carefully constructed ambush at a crossroads near Datchet with men hidden in gardens and houses each side of the railway track whilst one of the despatch riders using an 'Unexploded Bomb' notice ensured the convoy followed the target route. Once the leading cars had passed the crossing gate they were shut and the rear American cars 'shot up'. There followed a liberal use of smoke grenades much to the dismay of their target and his guards – "a few well-chosen explicit words made it clear – no more smoke" – but it proved a successful demonstration of capabilities and enthusiasm.[52]

Exercises provided a break from the unit's more normal daily duties and the meticulously completed diaries provide the most detailed account of the activities carried out by the mobile detachment over the months that followed. At the end of October 1940 Morris had driven his own car to conduct a "a special reconnaissance" accompanied by Thompson from the Coats Mission, most likely to

48 Ibid., pp.127-128
49 'Memories of the Coats Mission', Darell Papers
50 Day, 'The Coats Mission', p.9
51 Harwood, *Chivalry and Command*, p.122
52 'Memories of the Coats Mission', Darell Papers; 'Obituary – Brigadier Sir Jeffrey Darell', *The Daily Telegraph*, 29 March 2013

Newby Hall as they also called at Sandringham on the way back to Windsor. Sandringham was visited again at the end of November, presumably in readiness for the Christmas visit.[53] December saw further revisions to the detachment's vehicles with the arrival of the first two Humber staff armoured staff cars with bullet-proof windows and two new Norton 500cc side valve motor cycles. For the visit to Sandringham by the Royal Family two of the Guy armoured vehicles, one Humber, a brand new Fordson 30cwt lorry and three motor-cycles were initially sent to Norfolk although one of the vehicles had to be replaced whilst on route.[54] These were joined later by a replacement Guy, another of the Humbers and two more motor-cycles.

According to the nominal roll, and not including Captain Morris, at the year's end there were still just twelve men from the Lancers in the detachment supported by ten more from the Corps of Military Police. They were responsible for an impressive fleet of vehicles, two Guys, four Humbers, the original Lanchester, two of the 30cwt lorries, nine Nortons and four other motorcycles. Coats himself arrived at Sandringham on 8 January 1941 to relieve Morris who had helped drive one of the armoured cars back to Windsor. This was so it could be handed in at Slough and replaced with a new Humber Pullman Protected limousine, another bespoke vehicle designed specifically for VIP protection which was driven back to Norfolk on 10 January where it was demonstrated to the Royal Family two days later.[55] With Britain blanketed in heavy snow, a despatch rider who set off from Windsor on 18 January took two days to reach Sandringham and spent much of his time travelling across fields as the roads become impassable.[56] The weather was not the only concern, a single Dornier carried out another audacious air attack on the Royal Family dropping two bombs on 20 January only 300 yards from York Cottage but there were no casualties. The new Humber was used throughout the month as the King and Queen visited various aerodromes including Duxford and Mildenhall before they returned to central London on 30 January by train; the Pullman was there to transport them back to Windsor Castle. The following day the entire troop was inspected at Bushey by the King in what appears to have been his first visit to the Coats Mission's headquarters.

It was not only the Royal Family who used the vehicles. Another car was permanently based at Wellington Barracks at the disposal of the Prime Minister with two of the Lancers who had been detached from the main body. Its secondary purpose was to transport Cabinet ministers from their residences to the Cabinet War Room for meetings which often took place at night and during air raids. The driver had to face the challenge of driving around London "in the dark

---

53 Morris Detachment Diary, November 1940, 12th Lancers Archives, 912L: 2088/45, DMAG
54 Ibid., December 1940
55 Ibid., January 1941
56 Day, 'The Coats Mission', p.6

with limited vision and restricted sidelights in some of the heaviest raids".[57] There were also special visitors who required escorting, as in the first week of February 1941 when Morris drove the Pullman to collect the American politician Wendell Wilkie from Heston airfield and transport him to Windsor whilst the troop carried out an exercise near Epping Forest. The detachment was also continuing to expand with 13 more men arriving drawn from a variety of units including 17/21st Lancers, 1st East Riding Yeomanry, 27th Armoured Brigade, 1st Fife and Forfar Yeomanry, the Dragoon Guards, 15/19th and 16/5th Lancers and the 4/7th Hussars; within a few weeks they had all been transferred into the XII Lancers.[58]

The Royal visit to Scotland the following month again involved the Morris Detachment. The Pullman was driven up on 3 March and took two days to travel the 405 miles from Windsor to Glasgow, but was at the city's rail station in good time to meet the Royal Train. Supported by at least two of the other armoured staff cars these transported the King from Glasgow to Edinburgh and then on to Glamis Castle where he stayed for two nights before finishing his visit at Dundee.[59] By the beginning of April all of the Guys had been replaced and two Pullmans were sent to Sandringham the following week for the Easter visit.[60] The diary noted that six Thompson sub-machine guns were received in the first week of May to complete the establishment and the remainder of the month consisted of further re-organisation (including giving up responsibility for the prime minister's car) and accompanying a series of visits including Chatham and Brighton.[61] June involved further inspections across the Home Counties, and one of the Pullmans being moved to Newcastle by train where it was later joined by an armoured car. Based at Lord Ridley's House at Blagdon these were to accompany the King and Queen's Northern Tour which visited a number of important shipyards. For the remainder of the detachment they visited the home of Captain Morris in Heathfield, Sussex in two parties, where they embarked upon several days of hay-making.[62] There were more visits the following month, back to Sandringham and also to Salisbury Plain. Having attended the Passing Out Parade at Sandhurst on 1 August 1941, the Queen travelled to Glamis Castle in the middle of the month with the two Princesses.[63] Morris, along with a Pullman and an armoured car supported by one of the lorries and two despatch riders, had already headed to Scotland to arrange her protection; this group, the

57 Morris Detachment Diary, September 1940, 12th Lancers Archives, 912L: 2088/45, DMAG; Morris, 'The Morris Detachment', p.22; Trooper V. Cobley drove the small armoured car used by the Prime Minister
58 Morris Detachment Diary, February 1941, 12th Lancers Archives, 912L: 2088/45, DMAG
59 Ibid., March 1941; Arthur Erskine (The Crown Equerry) to Captain W.A. Morris, 28 February 1941, 912L: 2089/34
60 Ibid., Morris Detachment Diary, April 1941, 912L; 2088/45
61 Ibid., May 1941
62 Ibid., June/July 1941; Erskine to Morris, 14 June 1941, 912L: 2089/34
63 Ibid., August 1941, 912L: 2088/45

commanding officer plus eight other ranks and their vehicles, was referred to as 'Morris Detachment A'.[64] Morris was joined three days later by the remainder of his men as the King also arrived. The party now moved on to Balmoral Castle where they remained until returning to Windsor the following month.

A detailed inventory was also produced at this point which highlighted just how this force had expanded. In mid-August 1941 the Morris Detachment consisted of two officers, a staff sergeant and another sergeant, four corporals, 27 troopers, 10 motor cyclists attached from the military police, two cooks, 19 tradesmen, including nine mechanics, and 12 non-tradesmen which included the officers' batmen. This made for a total of 78 men.[65] For transporting the Royal Family there were four Humber Armoured Cars, three Pullman 'Protected' staff cars, and two Special Ironsides; it was hoped that the Humbers would soon be replaced by the Mark I Daimlers and that some additional Pullmans could be secured from 820 Company RASC which had more than ten of them although there was a need for these to be tested to see if they would "stand up to .503-in. fire". The main convoy was supported by three lorries carrying the baggage, blankets, food, reserve ammunition, anti-gas clothing and the cooks. There were a further two utility cars, two motorcycles for the detachment and the 10 motorcycles for the military police. Amongst the troops they had 35 pistols for personal protection and 12 Thompson sub-machine guns with nearly 8000 rounds of ammunition carried on them or in their vehicles. In addition there were eight BESA machine-guns, including the heavier 15mm version, and five more light machine-guns; in total there was nearly 24,000 rounds of ammunition available for these weapons. Finally, there were eight smoke dischargers and 48 rounds for them to be used if the convoy needed to try and evade capture. When added to the equipment carried by the Coldstreamers this would have made for a potent force which was well equipped for tackling a lightly armed opponent.

A well-rehearsed routine had been established and the men knew their roles but, in August 1941, an unusual issue had arisen when it was confirmed that Morris was next on the regimental promotion list: the concern was that it would be difficult to justify his appointment as a major responsible for such a small detachment.[66] The King himself instructed that no obstacle be placed in the way of Morris being promoted but at the same time it was also made clear that he wished him to remain in command. As Joey Legh wrote to the Home Forces Headquarters, "it would be difficult to exaggerate [the Morris Detachment's] importance in the event of an emergency".[67] There had been considerable efforts made to ensure secrecy, both in terms of the mobile element of the force and

64 Ibid., 'GHQ Home Forces Special Instruction "C"', 7 August 1941, 912L: 2089/34
65 Ibid., 'The Morris Detachment: War Establishment – Provisional', 13 August 1941
66 Brigadier C.G. Nicholson (General Headquarters, Home Forces) to Legh, 14 August 1941, WO199/297, TNA
67 Ibid., Legh to Major General A.E. Nye, 18 August 1941

also the Coats Mission, and there were clearly concerns about selecting the right officer. The greatest worry, however, was that any replacement would need to visit the various 'localities' that had been selected as refuges and it was feared that this would prejudice their security. The conclusion therefore was that any change in officer personnel would not be desirable and it was very much hoped that Morris would remain in his current post. This request was, not surprisingly, accepted and the necessary changes made. The Morris Detachment's diary was increasingly brief from this point although it noted the Christmas visit to Sandringham once more and listed the nominal strength at the end of 1941 as two officers, with the now Major Morris in command, supported by nine NCOs and 24 troopers along with 10 motor-cyclists still attached from the military police.[68] This was the final list as decisions had already taken place which would result in major changes to how the Royal Family were protected.

Lieutenant Colonel Francis Lane Fox, who had taken command of the Household Cavalry Training Regiment in June 1941, was adamant that the protection of the sovereign should now revert back to being the responsibility of his troops. Although he understood that the Household Cavalry would want to "carry out their peacetime duties in war", Morris clearly believed that his detachment had done a good job and there was a little reluctance from him to see the role end. He was prepared nonetheless to recommend that once these potential replacements, then in the process of being mechanised, were fully trained and equipped, the change should take place. If this were to happen he asked that Lord Birdwood could arrange for him and all his men to remain together and re-join their original regiment. In responding the Field Marshal, noting that he had not been informed about the Mission's progress for some time, confirmed he also was aware of the proposals and had been asked to "arbitrate" about who should have the responsibility.[69] This had led to him discussing the matter with Lane Fox who had been forced to concede that it would still be some time before his men were in a position to take over the Morris Detachment's duties and it was eventually agreed that on 4 December 1941 the mobile protection role would pass to the Household Cavalry. It would actually be 1 May the following year when the formal transfer took place.[70] This meant that the Lancers remained at their posts and when the time came for them to leave the men were not posted to a reinforcement camp but kept together allowing them to travel to the Middle East where some of them later fought in the final Battle of El Alamein.[71]

68 Morris Detachment Diary, December 1941, 12th Lancers Archives, 912L: 2088/45, DMAG; ibid., Alexander to Morris, 23 December 1941, 912L: 2089/34
69 Ibid., Birdwood to Morris, 23 October 1941
70 Lieutenant Colonel Francis Fox Lane to Headquarters (A) London District, 30 September 1941, WO199/297, TNA; ibid., Legh to Gregson-Ellis, 4 December 1941; Gregson-Ellis to Lieutenant-Colonel H.R. Norman, 23 January 1942; Birdwood to Morris, 18 December 1941, 12th Lancers Archives, 912L: 2089/34, DMAG
71 Gregson-Ellis to Legh, 3 December 1941, WO199/297, TNA

This grainy picture taken by a photographer from London District is the only reference that exists to the final inspection carried out by the Royal Family.

Aside from a visit to Ripon and aerodromes in the surrounding area in March, there is nothing else recorded in terms of activity conducted by the Morris Detachment throughout the early months of 1942, an indication of the decreasing role it was now playing as its duties were transferred to the Household Cavalry.[72] The final entry was dated 9 May – although the few published accounts point to it having been the following day – when all the men formed up in the inner quadrangle of Windsor Castle at 10am to be inspected by the King and Queen and the Princesses.[73] The two officers, Acting Staff Sergeant Major Thurston and two of the troopers were decorated with personal honours from the King and with this final act the Morris Detachment was disbanded and all of its remaining vehicles and equipment transferred to the Household Cavalry. The initial commanding officer of what still continued to be referred to as the Morris Detachment for a short period was Major Henry Garnett, who was not fit for service overseas, and his deputy was Lieutenant Roger Hall. The new commander did not appear to make a big impression on those around him, indeed one of the men who

72 Morris Detachment Diary, March 1942, 12th Lancers Archives, 912L: 2088/45, DMAG
73 'Memories of the Coats Mission', Darell papers; Morris Detachment Diary, May 1942, 12th Lancers Archives, 912L: 2088/45, DMAG; Morris, 'The Morris Detachment', p.23

transferred into the unit mistakenly believed that Hall was in charge.[74] As for Morris, the only officer in the entire Coats Mission to see the King and Queen on a daily basis, he left for his new posting with Birdwood's congratulations for the great honour he and his men had brought to his regiment.[75]

With the transfer of 'special duties' having been completed, the opportunity was also taken to review the unit's establishment to establish if it was adequately equipped.[76] This led to the proposal that there be an increase of eight personnel, the removal of the two "Special Ironside Saloons" which were not being used and the addition of four Daimler Mark II Scout Cars; this would mean there were now also four two-pounder guns available as the previous armoured cars had only carried machine guns. It was also proposed that the officer commanding be given a new four-seater Ford wheeled vehicle which would have an additional wireless in it and allow him to control the two combined patrols of two scout and two armoured cars which always preceded the unit when it moved. By July the changes had been made making the detachment, in theory, a more independent and batter armed force. At the end of December, with the disbandment of the Coats Mission, the light ambulance and medial officer's orderly were also transferred to the mobile force although this never actually took place and these were dispensed with entirely.[77] In December Lane Fox proposed that Lord Sefton take command but the idea was rejected by Legh, who appeared to retain considerable influence in the making of key decisions, and the following month the promoted Major Hall took charge of what, at the King's personal request, had now been re-named as the Household Cavalry Detachment.[78]

The previously discussed April 1943 review of the whole of Coats Mission extended to the Household Cavalry Detachment, and its strength was once again changed so that there were now two officers and 51 other ranks. It was also proposed that various contingencies be considered in terms of the response to particular types of threat.[79] In the event of what was termed 'Emergency 1', and with ample warning having been received and an extremely remote possibility of it coming under attack whilst on route, it was felt that a small, fast and lightly protected convoy would be desirable.[80] This would involve eleven vehicles in total along with six supporting motorcycles. In this configuration a scout car and five of the outriders would lead after which there would be an interval of about a mile before another scout car, along with both an armoured and a staff car, led

74 Day, 'The Coats Mission', p.3
75 Interview with Darell, 18 August 2010; Birdwood to Morris, 11 May 1942, 12th Lancers Archives, 912L: 2089/34, DMAG
76 GHQ Home Forces to Under-Secretary of State, War Office, 17 May 1942, WO199/291, TNA
77 Ibid., GHQ Home Forces to Under-Secretary of State, War Office, 30 December 1942, 16 January 1943
78 Legh to Gregson-Ellis, 13 December 1942, WO199/297, TNA; ibid., Legh to Lieutenant Colonel The Hon. James Hennessy, 13 January 1943
79 Ibid., Major R.W. Hall to GHQ Home Forces, 14 April 1943
80 'GHQ Operation Instruction, Special No.A', 3 April 1943, WO199/292, TNA

the way for the three protected saloons carrying the Royal Family, plus a police car and another car for the servants. At the rear of the convoy there was an armoured car and a scout car and one final motorcyclist. The other possibility, 'Emergency 11', was for if stronger protection were needed and would involve a slower but slightly larger moving convoy, the same as the first version but with nine extra vehicles carrying additional manpower and equipment. At the same time there was a duty section constantly available at instant readiness consisting of an armoured car and a scout car supported by two of the motorcycles as well as separate arrangements for the Protected Saloons which were also available at all times. In June 1943 what was termed as the 'Slow Convoy' was changed to ten vehicles with the addition of two more police cars provided by the Commissioner of the Metropolitan Police.[81]

Hall remained in the role until the summer of 1944 when he was replaced by Major The Hon. A.M. Baillie, another older officer who was unfit for active service, allowing him to be posted overseas.[82] Whilst the Chiefs of Staff Appreciation of October of that year decided that the houses and the dedicated force that was to protect them were no longer needed, the Household Cavalry Detachment was not altered nor were the special guards provided at Sandringham and Balmoral removed.[83] In fact the detachment was only formally disbanded on VE Day and its personnel reverted back to the Training Regiment although not until the King had had an opportunity to see them personally.[84] Only the two Daimler Pullmans which had been used by him were left along with their two corporals who drove them and would remain in their posts until they were eventually de-mobbed and released from their military service. The idea that some form of specific protection for the Royal Family was needed had managed to last throughout almost the entire war.

81 Ibid., 'Amendment No.3 to GHQ Operation Instruction, Special No.A', 21 June 1943
82 Lieutenant Colonel H.E. Cowie to Legh, 22 August 1944, WO199/297, TNA
83 Colonel F.C. Drew to Alexander, 6 November 1944, WO199/293, TNA; ibid., Alexander to Drew, 11 November 1944
84 Minutes from London District, 18/27 May 1945, WO199/297, TNA

6

Royal Refugees

The Coats Mission existed to provide security and protection for the Royal Family whilst they were in their official residences, as they travelled around the country and also in the event of a worst case emergency which required more extreme measures. Despite all of the enhanced steps that had been taken it was not possible to anticipate every threat such as occurred in February 1941 when an intruder managed to hide in the Queen's private room at Windsor Castle and grabbed her ankles as she entered.[1] A deserter who had lost his family in the Blitz, he had been taken on as an electrician despite his references not having been checked and was given a pass. He was later judged to be mentally disturbed and although he proved no threat at the time it was a frightening experience which demonstrated that the protection available was not guaranteed; Lord Wigram, the castle's Deputy Constable, subsequently ordered that procedures be improved. In the summer of 1941 Wigram again wrote to Churchill's military assistant, General Hastings 'Pug' Ismay, to highlight his more general concerns about the protection available at Windsor Castle when the King and Queen were in residence.[2] He was worried that the Grenadier Guards detachment stationed there were to be withdrawn leaving security in the hands of the Home Guard battalion. Whilst he was "very proud" of the volunteer troops, they were working men who lived at various points away from the castle and he believed that in the event of an attack on the Royal Family they could be defenceless for up to 90 minutes. As it was, following a discussion with the Chief of the Imperial General Staff, it was confirmed that no such plan existed and the Windsor Castle Defence Company of the Grenadiers would continue to act as the guard. It was clear, however, that there remained considerable concerns amongst some of those closest to the King and Queen about the existence of a potential security threat.

A particular source of concern involved wartime visits to the Sandringham Estate on the Norfolk coast. During the winter of 1939 the Royal Family had made their annual Christmas visit but instructions had been given to the press that it was not to be reported until they had returned to London.[3] The following year, in mid-October 1940, the King had approached General Alan Brooke, commanding Home Forces, to ask about the possibility of repeating the visit. The advice given to him had been that it would be not advisable to do so for

---

1   Shawcross, *Queen Elizabeth*, p.533
2   Lord Wigram to General Hastings Ismay, 20 June 1941, CAB121/227, TNA
3   C.V. Usborne to 'the Press', 13 November 1939, CAB21/2637, TNA

On the Sandringham Estate Appleton House was a brick built property which had a total of 20 rooms including those for the servants. It stood alone and was surrounded by forested parkland making it an ideal location to be used by the Royal Family during the wartime years.

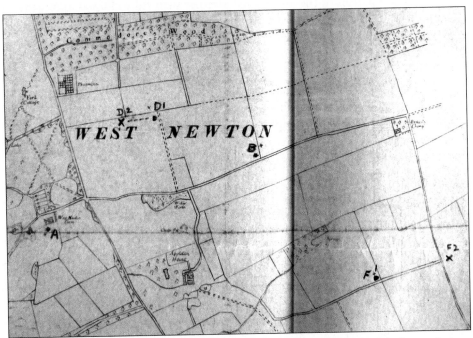

Map showing the locations of the six Bofors guns that were sited around the house during the summer 1942 visit to the Sandringham Estate. York Cottage, which was used by the officers of the Coats Mission, can be seen to the north-west of the house.

the remainder of that month as there was "reliable information of plans for an attempted invasion in the near future", but it should be safe him to travel from the middle of November onwards.[4] For the visit in December the main house was closed up and the Royal Family stopped at Appleton House, a smaller property on the estate which was a less obvious target to the German bombers. It also had the advantage of a large concrete bunker that had been built specially for their safety but was never actually used.[5] A specially procured commercial van travelled with the Morris Detachment on this occasion carrying the Royal Family's personal luggage along with "foodstuffs and other necessaries" that would be needed if an emergency arose requiring them to move immediately to their designated refuge.[6] That winter, which was one of the coldest of the century, there were snowball fights between the men and the Princesses and, when the lake froze over, an ice hockey match was organised in which Elizabeth took part and scored a goal.[7]

Details about the preparations for these visits to Sandringham were contained in 'GHQ Special Operation Instruction "D"'. In addition to troops from both the Mission and the Detachment there was also a flying column of troops. For the 1939 visit a company of infantry from the Royal Norfolk Regiment were stationed about a quarter of a mile away at York House and they, along with the Norfolk County Police and the permanently assigned detectives from the Metropolitan Police, were responsible for security.[8] One platoon was dug in around the house and conducted patrols of the area whilst another slept fully clothed and ready to move at very short notice. When available the troops from the 5th Battalion, the Norfolks carried out this role throughout the war but increasingly it fell to the other units often located at nearby Hillington Hall. On 29 December 1940 the much expanded guarding forces were inspected by the King, Queen and their two daughters and congratulated on a "good turnout".[9]

During the Royal Family's visit to Sandringham in the winter of 1941/42 the Coats Mission once again accompanied them. As Hancock recalled the protection plan now involved three platoons, one on duty, one ready to take over from them and the other resting. The estate water tower was also used as a daytime observation post.[10] There were also four Bofors anti-aircraft guns in the nearby trees.[11] With this level of protection Darell believed that Sandringham would have been safe but he also acknowledged that, although it would have only been possible in

4   Minute by Alan Brooke, 17 October 1940, WO199/287, TNA
5   'Obituary – Brigadier Sir Jeffrey Darell, Bt', *Norwich Evening News*, 12 March 2013; 'Memories of the Coats Mission', Darell Papers
6   Alexander to Lieutenant-Colonel G.P.L. Weston (GHQ Home Forces), 5 April 1943, WO199/293, TNA
7   'Memories of the Coats Mission', Darell Papers; 'Sutton man was King's bodyguard', *Ashfield Today*, 14 November 2006
8   Major General Bernard Paget to Alexander, 24 August 1940, WO199/287, TNA
9   Morris Detachment Diary, December 1940, 12th Lancers Archives, 912L: 2088/45, DMAG
10   'Obituary – Brigadier Sir Jeffrey Darell, Bt', *The Times*, 15 March 2013
11   Shawcross, *Queen Elizabeth*, pp.530-532

A copy of the letter sent by Princess Elizabeth thanking the men for her birthday gift.

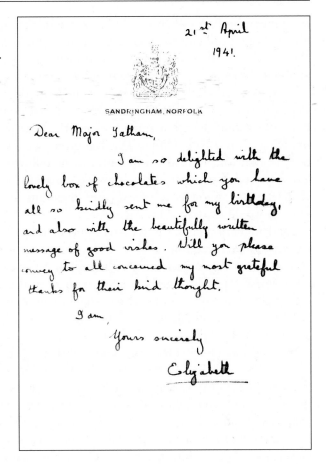

21st April 1941.

SANDRINGHAM, NORFOLK

Dear Major Jatham,

I am so delighted with the lovely box of chocolates which you have all so kindly sent me for my birthday, and also with the beautifully written message of good wishes. Will you please convey to all concerned my most grateful thanks for their kind thought.

I am,

Yours sincerely

Elizabeth

the dark, the flat country might well have still been suited for a German airborne attack.[12] In February 1942 additional security measures were put in place with repairs made to the existing barbed wire and more put around Appleton House which had previously been left clear at the King's request.[13] A number of small carefully concealed and camouflaged weapons pit were also placed around the house. Major Sir Ulick Alexander was concerned that this work might alert the Germans to the King's presence but he was reassured that there is "so much wire all over the country now that I don't think the small amount which will show from the air constitutes any great danger". For the September visit an additional mobile column was made available whilst the number of Bofors guns sited around Appleton House was increased to six.[14] The following summer some of the anti-aircraft guns were re-positioned at the King's request as they interfered with

---

12 Interview with Darell, 18 August 2010
13 Gregson-Ellis to Alexander, 10 February 1942, WO199/295, TNA
14 Ibid., Minute by Gregson-Ellis, 22 September 1942

the game shooting; in February 1944 some of the barbed wire was moved as it was making it difficult to tackle a threat from rabbits which were destroying the gardens.[15] Once the Coats Mission had been disbanded an infantry detachment of about the same size drawn from units training locally, three officers and 125 other ranks, provided the security. For the Christmas 1942/1943 visit this came from the King's Own Scottish Borderers, the following August it was provided by 5th Canadian Division and a few months later, in October, it was men from the King's Royal Rifle Corps. This last group were deemed to be so effective in the role that they were asked to repeat it the following month and for the entire festive period. Code-words were now also provided for the Royal Family's visits; all related correspondence was to use 'Pheasant' for the subject, and the local security would be termed as 'Force K'.[16]

Sandringham visits seem in many respects to have been a fairly relaxed experience with invitations for the officers to go and have tea and dinner with the King and Queen at Appleton House.[17] The military men noted how the Royal Family lived very simply during these stays with only the Queen's Equerry, Captain Campbell, in attendance. Hancock noted "how kindly and understanding" his hosts were which left their guards feeling "so very much at ease with them"; for her fifteenth birthday on 21 April 1941 which was celebrated at Sandringham, a card and box of chocolates was sent to Princess Elizabeth from all of the men in the Coats Mission. On Sundays all of those present would attend the little church, "the Royal Family walked there, we walked up there, there was no formality and even then Queen Elizabeth was famous for her lovely smile and we appreciated those times very much".[18] And on the first Sunday of each visit the King and Queen inspected the men beforehand and at the end of the service and had drinks with the officers and NCOs in York Cottage; according to Darell it was during the first of these informal receptions their host referred to them. Also at Sandringham, during the winter 1941/1942 visit, some of the troops accompanied the Royal shooting parties, acting as beaters; a high ranking general who had been invited to take part complained about the soldiers being used in this role to which the King responded, "General, I seem to have to remind you who owns and is Commander-in-Chief of the Army".[19] It is clear that these visits to Norfolk were popular not just for the Royal Family but also for the men guarding them. An examination of local mail in the first week of January 1943 revealed references to the presence of the King and Queen but the indiscretions were minor and the

15 Ibid., 'Report on visit to site "A" by G.S.O.II (A.A.)', 1 September 1943; Brigadier L. Bootle-Wilbraham (Eastern Command) to Lieutenant Colonel B.H. Churchill (GHQ Home Forces), 13 February 1944
16 Ibid., General Staff, Eastern Command, 'Subject – Special Visits', 19 September 1943
17 'Memories of the Coats Mission', Darell Papers
18 Interview with Hancock, 1984, IWM
19 'Memories of the Coats Mission', Darell Papers

general impression was that "the countryside is pleased to have the Royal Family in residence, as it reminds them of old times".[20]

Security was also inevitably a key consideration for visits to Balmoral. Having stayed in London the previous year as the Battle of Britain was fought in the skies over the capital, in August 1941 it was confirmed that the Royal Family intended once again to travel Scotland.[21] Following some discussions it was agreed that in order to offset any potential danger from bombing attacks or a sudden raid by German airborne troops, a considerable force would need to be provided. As has been seen, in addition to the Morris Detachment there was also an infantry battalion from Scottish Command – with one company guarding the site and another placed in readiness nearby – and an additional battalion held at Aberdeen in a reinforcing role. Men from the locally based units were quartered in the stables with the officers using the Garden Bungalow and Abergeldie Castle.[22] Up until 1942 whenever Balmoral was occupied additional patrols were carried out by Auxiliary Units drawn from across Scotland and Northumberland including the Lovat Scouts which provided an additional layer of security monitoring the castle's grounds.[23] These elite Home Guard units were tasked with conducting a guerrilla campaign were the country to have been invaded and occupied, but they fortunately found themselves with little to do other than carry out training exercises and these Royal visits provided an excellent opportunity to practise their skills. Well-trained in carrying out commando type operations, their role was "moving around in the darkness to strengthen and to test the guard at the castle".[24] The Ministry of Home Security was also able to supply sufficient police officers "for anti-sabotage measures" whilst Anti-Aircraft Command provided four Bofors guns and their crews. The Chiefs of Staff were in full agreement that not to have such measures "would be running an unjustifiable risk" particularly in light of the danger of a surprise airborne attack.[25]

The level of protection at the Scottish residence, certainly in the latter years of the war, was impressive. A typical disposition was that made available for the 1944 visit from August to September when, in addition to the Household Cavalry Detachment and the close protection provided by the Metropolitan Police, the special guard organised by Scottish Command consisted of an infantry battalion, 5th Battalion The Manchester Regiment (the headquarters and one full strength company), supported by a light anti-aircraft troop and a full fighter squadron.[26]

20 'Report on Snap Mail Examined 4-6 January 1943', 11 January 1943, WO199/295, TNA
21 C.G.G. Nicholson to Commander Collis, 21 July 1941, CAB121/227, TNA
22 Minute from G(Ops) to D.C.G.S., 16 July 1942, WO199/294, TNA
23 Ibid.
24 David Lampe, *The Last Ditch: Britain's Secret Resistance and the Nazi Invasion Plan* (London; Greenhill Books, 2007), p.111
25 Ismay to Hardinge, 23 July 1941, CAB121/227, TNA
26 Minute by GHQ Home Forces, 3 August 1944, WO199/294, TNA; ibid., Churchill to Legh, 2 August 1944; 'LAA – Special Deployment', 31 July 1944; Minute by Southern Command, 23 July 1944

Other troops in the vicinity who were training would also be made aware that they might be required as reinforcements. The Manchesters had previously been carrying out marshalling and traffic control duties in Southern Command as part of the operations connected with the Allied Invasion of Europe. In April 1944 in the run up to the Normandy invasion the continuing burden imposed by having to provide additional guards for Sandringham and Balmoral had been reviewed. There was only one infantry unit available, 52 Division which was earmarked for an air-landing role in support of any future airborne operations. As the minute on the subject noted "the paucity of troops under Home Forces in future makes it desirable to consider the extent to which the degree of protection afforded up to the present will be necessary". Only one copy of this document was prepared for General Sir Harold Franklyn, who had been appointed as Commander-in-Chief Home Forces in January 1944, but he decided that the required guards would have to be found.[27] It was clear, however, that it was becoming progressively more difficult to find the additional manpower needed to fill this role but it continued until the visit to Sandringham which concluded on the final day of April 1945 and the following month it was confirmed that there would only be a police guard required in future.[28]

Providing security at the principal Royal residences was in many respects the secondary role for the Coats Mission. Its primary purpose for which it had been established in the summer of 1940 was to evacuate the Royal Family away from the properties they normally used in the event of their being a threat to their security, but there has remained a lot of uncertainty about the exact details of what this actually would have entailed. According to Princess Margaret, who was not told about the plans until long after the war, "there was a line of [country houses] … we were to be shunted from one to the other until we reached Liverpool".[29] Another account refers to the Royal Family being moved to Holyhead in Wales from where the Royal Navy would have transferred them to Canada, although Southampton was also mentioned as a possibility.[30] The post-war official history of the Coldstream Guards published in 1951 also referred to there being four houses although it did not name them.[31] Confirming that at the time very few knew all of the details, even Darell, as one of the platoon commanders who was briefed fully on Coats' intentions and was involved in the June 1940 recce, could only recall three houses.[32] Although he never knew the name, he believed

27 'Protection of His Majesty the King against Enemy Airborne or Seaborne attack', April 1944, Not Sent, WO199/295, TNA

28 Ibid., Legh to Major-General C.B. Callender, 7 April 1945; 'Telephone Record', 19 May 1945

29 Conversation with author, cited in Aronson, *The Royal Family at War*, p.30

30 'A fascinating but little-known piece of British history', 'Sixth Army Group', January 2010, http://www.sixtharmygroup.com/portal/viewtopic.php?t=21314&sid=dfef6a6ebd0a305097fc40 3d19d77003

31 Howard and Sparrow, *The Coldstream Guards*, p.21

32 'Memories of the Coats Mission', Darell Papers; Howard and Sparrow, *The Coldstream Guards*, p.21

Madresfield Court in Worcestershire is the ancestral home of the Lygon family. A feudal castle that dated from before the 1120s when it was mentioned in the charter of Henry I, it had a double moat and 162 rooms. It was also in a remote location between the Malvern Hills and the River Severn making it an ideal location for a Royal refuge.

the fourth had been compromised and his reminiscences suggest that this was Croome which had been removed in May 1940 prior to his arrival. Despite his position as Assistant Director of Works at GHQ Home Forces and the knowledge this gave him of the Coats Mission, even Harry Hopthrow was later only absolutely sure of the name of one of the refuges; he thought that Chatsworth in Derbyshire might have been another and believed there to be a third site but did not know the details.[33] Yet the June 1943 amendment to the operation instruction referred to their being four "selected residences" which suggests that in the interim the numbers had been increased.[34] Notes prepared in the 1960s by HQ London District offered the most concise description of the role.[35] This described it as being "protecting the persons of the Royal Family in any one of four houses in different parts of the country, and conveying them to or from these houses with a Mobile Column".[36]

33   Interview with Harry Hopthrow, Catalogue Number 11581, 1990, Reel 23, IWM

34   'Amendment No.3 to GHQ Operation Instruction, Special No.A', 21 June 1943, WO199/292, TNA

35   'Protection of the Royal Family in War', Commander J.R. Stephens RN, 2 April 1965, WO32/21796, TNA; these were used for reference when considering the role of the post-war equivalent

36   Day, The Coats Mission'

It is not clear who was responsible for selecting these residences but there is good reasons to believe that Coats himself was involved choosing refuges that were known both to him and his charges and were owned by friends who often had connections with the Coldstream Guards. His wife's aunt, Lady Evelyn Gordon-Lennox, who was married to Sir John Cotterell and whose son Richard married into the Lygon family, was an example of the vast network known to this influential officer. Through this connection very likely came the link to Madresfield Court in Worcestershire, a feudal castle that dated from before the 1120s when it was mentioned in the charter of Henry I. This remote property had a double moat and 162 rooms, 54 of which were bedrooms, and was in an anonymous location at the heart of the hamlet which bears its name. In terms of mounting a defence it would seem to have been an excellent choice allowing the Royal Family to be moved to a largely hidden site to the east of the Malvern Hills and west of the River Severn.[37]

The 8th Earl and Lady Beauchamp at Madresfield.

At the start of the Second World War it was the home of William Lygon who in November 1938, at the age of just 35 years old, became the 8th Earl Beauchamp after the death of his controversial father. The Lygon family had already lived there for several hundred years when in 1815 William Lygon was created the first Earl of Beauchamp. The most infamous of those to follow him was the Seventh Earl who was forced into exile in 1931 after his homosexuality became known by King George V, events that were

---

37 It is also the only one of the refuges which has generated any recent interest in terms of the potential wartime role for which it was earmarked. Zoe Chamberlain, 'Secret war plan for Royal Family to be evacuated to Worcester', *Sunday Mercury*, 17 January 2011; Neil Tweedie, 'Madresfield Court: The King's redoubt if Hitler called', *Daily Telegraph* (London), 19 January 2011; Ben Fenton, 'A Brideshead hideaway for princesses at war', *Daily Telegraph* (London), 10 January 2006

immortalised by Evelyn Waugh in his novel 'Brideshead Revisited' which was based on the family and its ancestral home.[38] Educated at Eton and Magdalen College, Oxford, the Eighth Earl had previously been a Liberal member of parliament with a Norfolk constituency and for a number of years served Leslie Hore-Belisha in the National government as his Parliamentary Private Secretary. He was apparently fully committed to his political role and an active member of the House of Lords where he sat on a number of committees; he was also heavily involved in local Worcestershire affairs acting as a County Councillor and, following the war, a Deputy Lieutenant.[39] As soon as the war had started he joined the Royal Army Ordnance Corps and was stationed at Didcot in Oxfordshire. Lady Beauchamp – the Danish heiress Else Schiwe whose previous property millionaire husband had died unexpectedly and who he had married in June 1936 – joined him here every weekend.

In March 1939 Madresfield Court was listed in the pre-war official 'Central Register of Accommodation', which was maintained by the Office of Works, as having been earmarked as a potential War Office hospital in the event of war. This was because Earl Beauchamp, who did not know the plans at this stage, had offered the hall for these purposes, but it was removed from the official requisitioning lists at some stage later in the summer with no reason being given as to why this had been done.[40] Lady Beauchamp confirmed that when asked why the house was not being used for any apparent official business one of the reasons given was that it continued to be reserved for a future medical role. In an interview in 1989 she recalled that it was "very difficult. Everybody was so curious. They asked me all the time questions about it. Why are you all alone in that big house, with your 54 bedrooms? So first I tell them that it was going to be a convalescent home. But then the army, they made big defences here. So I said, you mustn't say to anyone, but the treasures from the Tower of London are coming".[41] According to her recollections it was to be used by the two Princesses – 'treasures from the tower' – for whom two bedrooms were kept prepared, one in pink and the other in blue.[42] Their potential hosts placed a book on their prospective bedside tables appropriate to their age which was changed annually.[43] Lady Beauchamp kept

38 Richard Greenway, *The Story of Madresfield Court* (Malvern; First Paige, 1991); Jane Mulvagh, 'Evelyn Waugh: A blueprint for Brideshead', *Daily Telegraph*, 24 May 2008; John de la Cour, 'Madresfield Court', Elmley Foundation
39 Selina Hastings, 'House of Memories', *The Spectator*, 2 September 2009
40 Sir Patrick Duff to the Clerk to the County of Worcestershire, 29 June 1939 (Worcestershire County Archives); with its reference number of '57923' the name is struck through in pencil and moved to Addendum 32 where it is formally listed as having been deleted
41 Hastings, 'House of Memories'
42 Ibid.
43 Paula Byrne, *Mad World – Evelyn Waugh and the Secrets of Brideshead* (London; Harper Press, 2009), p.271; a list exists at the house showing the names of who would stay in each bedroom

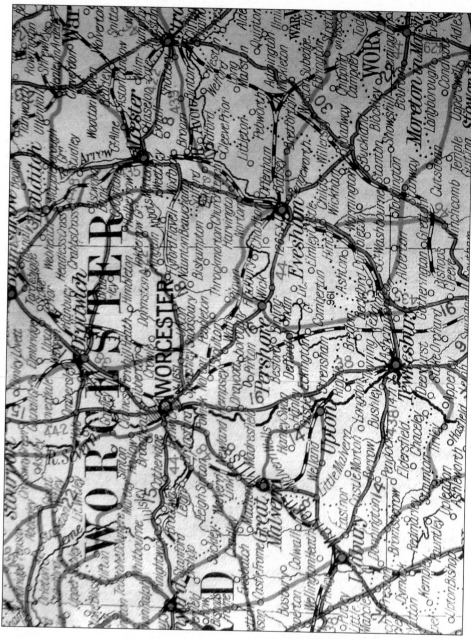

A period map showing Madresfield's location in relation to Worcester. Stratford-upon-Avon is just on the map's eastern edges; 'Defford', which is also marked was the location of Croome Court.

a room booked permanently in a hotel in nearby Malvern in case the King and Queen accompanied their daughters and she needed to leave.[44]

As has been discussed, Croome was most likely initially assigned the role and it appears that it was only following the security lapse that Madresfield Court was identified as the new 'Establishment "A"'. After the defeat of France "the possibility of the Royal Family evacuating to the West Country became a very likely event" and Corbitt, the Royal official who had been given the role of making the initial arrangements, received new instructions "to deal with the situation in the best way that I could for as long as it was necessary".[45] He was told that in the event of an emergency he would travel to the new site with the Queen and the two Princesses and remain with them whilst taking charge of the Household Supply Department.[46] Much as had been the case with Croome, a local grocer was vetted and had to sign the Official Secrets Act in anticipation of delivering fruit and vegetables to the Royal Family.[47] Food supplies were reportedly transported to the house following the war's outbreak in unmarked lorries and then stored in the cellars.[48] Despite the paramount need for secrecy, when a visit was made by officials from London to review the preparations that were being made they discovered that "somebody had plastered the doors of the different rooms ... with signs saying 'Her Majesty's Lady in Waiting' and so on".[49] Another of those involved recorded that Coats came in to see him one day at GHQ Home Forces furiously complaining that an advance party from the Royal Household had gone down to Madresfield Court to put in a skeleton staff and the first thing they had done was put the Royal letter box at the end of the drive.[50]

It is not clear if this was also noted by Chief Inspector Cameron when he and a senior officer from the Coats Mission visited Madresfield Court to examine its suitability.[51] As has been discussed, his May 1940 visit led to Sergeant Goodwill being appointed to protect the two Princesses.[52] It was confirmed to the young policemen that if the situation became worse the two girls were to be moved to Madresfield Court and the plan called for an additional four constables to also travel with the party in their own police vehicle and report for duty at the new location. In addition another sergeant and five constables were to accompany the King and Queen when they eventually left to join their children. Whilst these preparations were being made the military were also taking steps to strengthen

44 Hastings, 'House of memories'
45 Corbitt, *My Twenty Years in Buckingham Palace*, p.161
46 Research by Richard Beighton
47 Tweedie, 'Madresfield Court...', 19 January 2011
48 Fenton, 'A Brideshead hideaway...',10 January 2006; Chamberlain, 'Secret war plans...', 17 January 2011
49 David Birt, *The Battle of Bewdley* (Great Witley; Peter Huxtable Designs, 1988), p.10
50 Interview with Hopthrow, 1990, IWM
51 'Letters to Editor' (from Colin Bowden), *Malvern Gazette*, 28 January 2011
52 Minute by Chief Inspector H. Cameron (Canon Row, 'A' Division), 22 May 1940, MEPO3/1893, TNA

the site. Hancock, speaking some years after the event, recalled that in terms of preparations, each of the houses "had to be made into, as it were, a local fortress and it had to be done with the greatest secrecy".[53] This was a key element of the Mission's role and "it was absolutely vital that as few people as possible knew where they were and we had to be most careful, everything we did or said". Nonetheless steps had to be taken and it appears that some thought was given to defensive measures with a series of slit trenches placed at strategic points around the perimeter of the house and grounds so that they could not be seen from outside. There were plans for barbed wire entanglements but Hancock did not think they were actually put in place so "that nothing untoward should appear to be going on at these places". Periodically he and Tatham would visit the houses to see that the trenches had not fallen in and to make sure there were no obstructions to the selected route from Bushey.

Even before this work began, in March 1940 Colonel George Henderson had been posted to the headquarters of Western Command at Queen's Park in Chester as Chief Signal Officer. With the worsening war situation this was re-organised to cover a huge area running from Cumberland and the Isle of Man down to Worcestershire and the South Wales Area. Writing in 1966 the then retired brigadier claimed that when he had taken over his new appointment he had received a personal 'Top Secret' envelope marked 'The Rocking Horse'. This described how in the event of an invasion of Britain and the attacking German forces succeeding beyond a certain point, the Royal Family would be moved to a place of safety and, if the situation worsened further, they would be flown to Canada via Iceland. He went on to record how he reported to Madresfield Court with instructions to install telephones in most of the rooms along with additional switchboards and tele-printers and a connection to the local farmhouse where the escort – which he mistakenly described as Grenadier Guards – was stationed. He also put in additional lines to the Worcester GPO Exchange. As he acknowledged in his letter the equipment was never used and he returned subsequently to dismantle it.[54]

In addition to the preparations at the refuges made by specialists and the men of the Coats Mission, there were local defences organised separately and, at Madresfield Court, this responsibility fell to Lieutenant Colonel Rupert Melville-Lee who was Commanding Officer of the Worcestershire Regiment's

53 Interview with Hancock, 1984, IWM
54 The anecdote comes from a file held at the National Archives detailing Brigadier Henderson's enquiries about publishing the story in his autobiography. The Ministry of Defence conducted an investigation and could find no records, nor indeed any knowledge of such a plan, leading them to seek advice from the Cabinet Office on how to proceed. Ultimately it was confirmed that the Brigadier's wartime role should remain confidential and a warning should be sent to the writer that he would be committing a breach of the Official Secrets Act if he continued; Brigadier H.G. Henderson to Major General Bradley, 2 March 1966, CAB103/616, TNA; ibid., W.I. McIndoe (Cabinet Officer) to Major J. Bingham (Ministry of Defence), 9 May 1966

Newby Hall is country house near Ripon in Yorkshire that was built at some point between 1695-1705 for Sir Edward Blackett who came from a wealthy land-owning family and was a Member of Parliament for Ripon and, later, Northumberland. Possibly built to designs by Sir Christopher Wren, in 1940 there was both a family link to James Coats and it was known to the Royal Family.

Depot at Norton Barracks.[55] The two regular battalions were overseas so it was left to two territorial battalions, the 7th and 8th along with the 9th and 10th which were two newly formed battalions, to defend the county. All of these new recruits meant that while the infantry training centre had been designed to run a course for 400 men, the nature of the emergency meant that there was now an intake of approximately 3000 reporting for duty. From this group a small mobile column of 80 men, a dozen cars, two buses and two Bren gun carriers was kept permanently ready to respond to reports of enemy parachutists. These were supported by scattered troops manning lookout posts to report back to the depot in the event of an attack taking place. But there was also a 'secret job' the purpose of which was not disclosed to even the senior officers within the regiment. As part of a scheme prepared by Melville-Lee, which he also referred to as 'Rocking Horse', a force of troops was assembled to assist with the protection of "important figures or institutions". Sites included both Spetchley Manor, intended for the prime minister, and Madresfield Court which he was told "had been selected as a refuge for the Royal Family should it become necessary to hide them in an unexpected place". As the River Severn ran between the house and the barracks

55 Birt, *The Battle of Bewdley*, pp.9-10; Jeff Carpenter and Brian Owen, *Worcester at War* (Privately published, 1986), p.19; 'Lieut.-Colonel Rupert Henry MELVILLE-LEE', http://www.worcester-shireregiment.com/wr.php?main=inc/o_melville_lee

the colonel requisitioned a manor house on the far bank of the river and billeted within it a mobile force within easy reach of the refuge although the men were not apparently aware of the potential role they were to play. It is perhaps worth noting by way of conclusion, that in October 1941, the Malvern Home Guard conducted an invasion exercise which simulated a German airborne landing east of the River Severn. In this a small group of attackers had landed in Madresfield Park which "was considered to be an admirable ground for such an exercise" and ultimately the defending forces were overcome by a flanking attack.[56] It is hoped that members of the Coats Mission were observing or, at the very least, made aware of this outcome.

The most likely alternative (if, for whatever reason, it had not been possible to make use of Madresfield) was Newby Hall near Ripon in Yorkshire. Described as "one of the smaller country houses of Yorkshire", this had passed to Captain Edward Compton and his wife in 1921 although it had been in the same family since the mid-Eighteenth century.[57] There were various reasons for its selection as a possible refuge for the Royal Family. Most obviously Queen Elizabeth was an old family friend, whilst Captain Compton was a godson of King Edward VII. The Royal Family had also stayed at Newby Hall a number of times before the war.[58] In addition, at the war's outbreak, Edward Compton's brother Clare, a Royal Navy officer, who had succeeded to the neighbouring Studley Royal estate where the future King and Queen had also stayed, was the brother-in-law of Jimmy Coats.[59] The then Major Coats had in 1917 married Lady Amy Gordon-Lennox. Having legally changed his name in March 1912, the now Clare Vyner married Amy's younger sister, Lady Doris, in 1923 establishing the connection. The father-in-law of both men was Charles Gordon-Lennox, the 8th Duke of Richmond, the head of a distinguished family which had long established connections with British royalty.[60] As a final link a son was born to the Comptons, Robin, and in 1940 he was in the Coldstream Guards.

Coats visited the hall on the first day of July 1940 to confirm that arrangements were in order for its possible use. Both Captain Compton, who was in Edinburgh, and Mrs Compton, who was staying in London, were advised of this visit in a letter, presumably sent by the agent, who confirmed that arrangements had been made for the troops to be billeted in the stables which were described as "eminently suitable for the purposes required".[61] The house was also more generally being made

56 Mick Wilks, *Chronicles of the Worcestershire Home Guard* (Herefordshire; Logaston Press, 2014), pp.80-82

57 Sheena Hastings, 'The home guard (Newby Hall and Gardens)', *The Yorkshire Post*, 28 July 2013

58 Sarah Freeman, 'Secrets of the Royal refuge', *The Yorkshire Post*, 25 March 2013; Robert Hardman, 'Defending the real Downtown Abbeys', *The Spectator*, 9 March 2013

59 *Newby Hall – An Illustrated Survey of the Yorkshire Home of Compton Family* (Derby; English Life Publications, n.d./1953?)

60 'Goodwood House and the Duke of Richmond', *Britain Magazine*, 7 May 2009; 'Obituary – The Duke of Richmond', *The Times*, 8 May 1935

61 W. Dale to Captain Compton, 1 July 1940, Newby Hall Papers (Newby Hall, Yorkshire, kindly

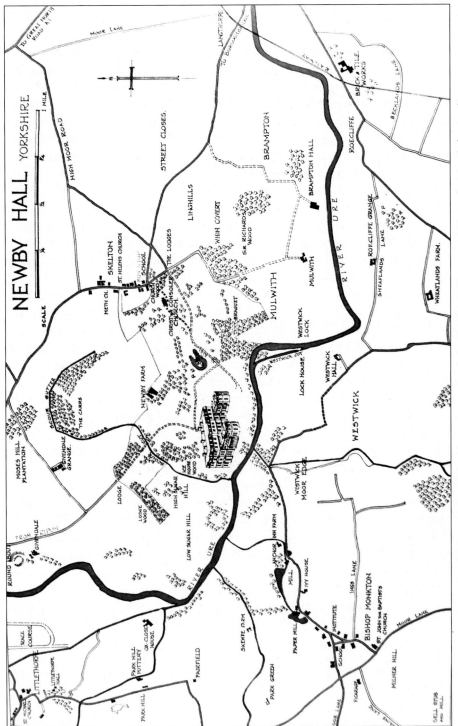

As with Madresfield Newby Hall had large grounds whilst the River Ure provided an obvious defensive line.

ready "for the visit of your guests" although there was already some reference to potential competition for accommodation with a note about the Servants' Wing and its possible use by Royal Air Force officers and senior NCOs from bomber crews stationed at nearby RAF Dishforth if their aerodrome was badly bombed.[62] The agent by this stage had been told he was to make preparations for "housing and accommodating a high government official under certain circumstances" although Captain Compton was still uncertain of the details. An undated note, almost certainly written in late June, detailed the arrangements required by Mrs Compton in advance of this "emergency visit".[63] There would be six hours' notice before the group's arrival at which point the Compton's own bedroom and one other were to be cleared of clothing and some of their ornaments while another six servants rooms were to be made available, one each for a detective, valet, chauffeur, ladies maid, kitchen maid and a house maid. Additional supplies were also to be bought including a ham, stilton cheese and some cream cracker biscuits and a dozen bottles of hock or Chablis, two bottles each of sherry and whiskey and some soda.

As was the case at Madresfield a problem developed when the West Riding branch of the Red Cross made a request to visit the hall which Compton had offered as a convalescent home, presumably before it had been earmarked for its other potential role.[64] The approach was initially politely declined on the basis that Newby had "been reserved by the Ministry for their own purposes", although it was not made clear which ministry, whilst reference was also made to the proposed RAF use of the servants' quarters.[65] The County Director of the Red Cross, Lieutenant-Colonel A.C. Sheepshanks DSO, who had been a Master at Eton before the war, wrote back and asked that he be allowed to inspect the hall. The Compton's agent had no choice but to agree although once again with a note that he did not believe it would be possible to transfer the building.[66] Having had another approach from other Billeting Officers for any available space, he also now wrote to Captain Compton asking for confirmation as to "how far I should go in explaining what [Newby Hall] is being reserved for".[67] The Red Cross party visited at the end of the first week of September 1940 and assured the agent that they would have precedence over "the Ministry".[68] Despite his confidence, within a week Sheepshanks had, however, written back to confirm that Newby Hall was now not suitable as a convalescent home although the Red

supplied by David Winpenny) (hereafter 'NH'); ibid., Dale to Mrs E Compton, 1 July 1940. It is perhaps worth noting that the agent felt it necessary to mention that "Major Coates (sic) was Clare Vyner's brother-in-law"

62 'Newby Hall and the Coats Mission'; again with grateful thanks to David Winpenny for his notes
63 'Mrs Comptons requests rooms be got ready…', n.d., NH
64 Ibid., Lieutenant Colonel A.C. Sheepshanks (British Red Cross Society) to Dale, 29 August 1940
65 Ibid., Dale to Sheepshanks, 30 August 1940
66 Ibid., 3 September 1940
67 Ibid.
68 Ibid., Dale to Captain Compton, 7 September 1940

Cross did later store some goods in the granaries.[69] Lady Compton had apparently contacted the couple's friends within the Royal circle to ask for advice about how to proceed and whether it was possible to produce some form of official confirmation that the house was being held in reserve for the government. The response did not arrive until the following month, after the problem had already passed, when Major Sir Ulick Alexander, responsible for co-ordinating the Mission's activities with GHQ Home Forces, finally responded. Whilst apologising for the delay, he suggested the best answer was to say that the house had been reserved by the Commander-In-Chief Home Forces and all enquiries should be directed to him.[70] As he noted, it would be difficult to arrange anything else "without causing some suspicion". In the meantime preparations were made to defend the refuge with slit trenches placed at strategic points around both the house and the garden including a machine gun installed on the steps below the south side at the top of the herbaceous border.[71]

There is no further mention of Newby until the following summer when Majors Tatham and Hancock visited to inspect the house. They also told the agent that there "was still a possibility of the London people coming up here" possibly at short notice.[72] At the same time other attempts continued to be made to secure the use of the hall, and a visit in August 1941 from a Major Wood was the third from Northern Command's Headquarters. Despite being allowed to take measurements of certain rooms, he was told that the hall had been "earmarked for special purposes" and could not be used in any other role.[73] Major Compton replied to this latest update from his agent with his apologies that he was once again being bothered by visits which were "a complete waste of time". In December 1942, as the Coats Mission was stood down, orders were received to remove most of the defence works and return any secret papers back to HQ London District.[74] Two years later, in December 1944, arrangements were made for the remainder of the barbed wire defences to be taken down and the machine gun emplacements to be filled in and by the end of the following February this work had been completed.[75]

Madresfield Court and Newby Hall appear to have been the two principal sites chosen for the Royal role, and they were certainly where the greatest amount of preparation were made but there were also two other potential properties for emergency use. The June 1943 amendment to the operation instruction also

69 Ibid., 13 September 1940
70 Ibid., Ulick Alexander to (Eddy) Compton, 9 October 1940
71 Freeman, 'Secrets of the Royal refuge'
72 Dale to Major Compton, 25 June 1941, NH
73 Ibid., 7 August 1940
74 Freeman, 'Secrets of the Royal refuge'; 'Subject: Special Accn', Northern Command (York), 7 December 1944, NH
75 Alexander to Drew (GHQ Home Forces), 20 November 1944, WO199/293, TNA; ibid., 'Subject – Special Accommodation', 10 March 1945

provides the only exact confirmation of what, at this point, were the four 'selected residences' but which had, in all likelihood, remained the same since the Mission was first stood up three years before.[76] With the threat receding on an almost daily basis, Madresfield Court remained the first option and had been given the code-word 'Harbour' followed by Newby Hall, referred to as 'Security'. There was also Pitchford Hall in Shropshire, 'Refuge', and owned by General Sir Charles Grant, another distinguished Coldstream Guards officer who had only retired in 1940 from his final post as General Officer Commanding in Chief of Scottish Command and Governor of Edinburgh Castle. The property had been visited in April 1935 by the future King and Queen, a young Princess Victoria having also stayed there previously, and in the General's wartime absence his wife Lady Sybil Grant, the daughter of the former prime minister Lord Roseberry, was in charge.[77] Darell recalled that Lady Grant was rather eccentric and spent most of her time living in a house built in a tree in the garden.[78] Finally, there was Burwarton House, Viscount Boyne's home approximately seven miles south-west of Bridgnorth in Shropshire, which was given the code-word 'Peaceful'.[79] Little is known about it, or the proposed role and defences, other than it was visited in February 1943 by an agent enquiring about using it for billeting troops.[80] The commanding officer for Western Command, in which the house was located, was advised that the property was required for special purposes and no further inspections were to be made without securing prior permission from GHQ Home Forces.[81] These remained the four selected properties until November 1944 when the order was finally issued stating that accommodation "reserved for Special Purposes" was now no longer needed and could be de-requisitioned.[82] Whilst the Household Cavalry Detachment retained its role for another six months, to where it would have taken the Royal Family if an emergency had occurred was not clear.

76 'Amendment No.3 to GHQ Operation Instruction, Special No.A', 21 June 1943, WO199/292, TNA

77 'Pitchford Hall – Stately Treehouses, Old and New', in Anthony Aikman, *Treehouses* (Privately Published), pp.49-60; 'Obituary – Caroline Colthurst', *Daily Telegraph*, 28 January 2011; Jane Kelly, Heartbreak house', *Daily Mail* (London), 5 September 1992

78 'Memories of the Coats Mission', Darell Papers

79 'List of Selected Residences', n.d., WO199/293, TNA

80 Ibid., Alexander to Major-General J.A. Sinclair, 3 March 1943

81 Ibid., GHQ Home Forces to HQ Western Command, 4 March 1943

82 Ibid., 'Accommodation reserved for Special Purposes', 21 December 1944; 'Subject – Special Accommodation', 22 November 1944

7

A German Plan?

For five years preparations were made but nothing ever happend and the Coats Mission remained, thankfully, not needed. There was allegedly, however, a plan to attack Buckingham Palace at the outset of a German invasion of Britain in September 1940 the aim of which, exactly as some had feared at the time, was to capture and secure as hostages those members of the Royal Family who were present. The evidence remains difficult to substantiate coming as it does from a single source, Dr. Otto Begus, a German officer who claimed to be centrally involved. As the self-identified leader of this "dramatic story" he was interviewed in 1959 for a story published in the *Sunday Pictorial*, a sensationalist but extremely popular British weekend newspaper which at the time was attracting a readership of around five million people.[1] The writer was Comer Clarke, an investigative journalist who two years later also published a book which was one of the earliest to study what might have happened if Britain had been occupied and ruled by the Nazis.[2] This repeated the Begus story in a slightly expanded form but, since its publication, other references to this alleged plan are difficult to find. A much more recent examination of the same theme has also described "a daring plot to kidnap the leading members of the royal family during the early hours of an invasion".[3] The description of the "audacious conspiracy", taken almost entirely from the interview given by Begus, concludes that the chances of the plan succeeding would have been slim in large part due to the absence of many of its targets which it mistakenly claims had already been dispersed elsewhere. An earlier account was equally dismissive; having reviewed the 100 page printed handbook on Great Britain produced by the Gestapo, the *Informationscheft G.B.*, which was intended to act as a guide for the occupying German forces, this concluded that no reason could be seen to substantiate such a claim as there was no reference within the document to any plot.[4] This account did, however, note that the Gestapo were

1 Comer Clarke, 'Kidnap The Royal Family…', *The Sunday Pictorial*, March 22, 1959
2 Clarke, *England Under Hitler* (London; Consul Books, 1963). There is some suggestion that Clarke had intelligence connections and he appears to have split his research between plots relating to the Second World War and the Cold War. Enquiries about a will or details of his family and career proved unsuccessful beyond that he "had a reputation for selling sensational and sometimes spurious stories"; Anthony Summers, *Conspiracy* (New York; McGraw-Hill, 1980), p.364
3 Leo McKinstry, *Operation Sealion*, pp.230-232
4 Lampe, *The Last Ditch*, pp.32-33

particularly interested in the role of the Special Branch and the protection they afforded to the Royal Family.[5]

Further doubts about the plot stem from the credentials of Begus. He certainly belonged to a wartime organisation within the German military that had something of an elite status and was charged with conducting unusual missions. Post-war American intelligence summaries which described Begus as "completely untrustworthy" at the same time referred to him as "one of the top German intelligence agents during the last war".[6] His MI5 file makes no mention of his service in France, from where he claimed the plan was to be launched, instead concentrating on his subsequent activities in Greece and Italy.[7] There is, however, an intriguing reference to information received from General Walter Krivitskiy, a Soviet defector

The identification picture for Dr Otto Begus taken from one of his American intelligence files.

who was interviewed by MI5 in January 1940, which creates some doubt; whilst Begus was not named directly it was claimed that he potentially could have been in Britain at that point and passing himself off as a refugee.[8] Wartime intelligence at this stage was an often imprecise business with half-truths and repeated inaccuracies but the very fact that this relatively junior German officer was being monitored by the Russians reflected a possible significance.

The details of the proposed raid as dictated by Begus at his home near Salzburg in 1959 certainly made for exactly the kind of sensational story favoured by journalists. It was to be led by the then Captain (*Hauptsturmfuehrer*) Begus who had been born in September 1899 in Bozen in Austria – now Bolzano in Italy – and had served in the First World War during which he was wounded and captured on the Italian front.[9] Post-war, after completing his studies and qualifying as a doctor of laws, hence why the literature that does exist refers to him

5   Ibid., p.41
6   'Subject: BEGUS, Dr. Otto', May 1950, Security Classified Intelligence and Investigative Dossiers (National Archives and Records Administration, Maryland), RG319, Box 671
7   'Begus, Otto', KV2/527, TNA
8   Ibid., 'Extract from Information Obtained from General Krivitskiy, January-February 1940'
9   He was promoted Major in September 1943; SS Number – 189613; Nazi Party number – 3354998

as Dr. Begus, he eventually became a police official in Austria but was arrested due to his National Socialist sympathies.[10] From a very early stage in its development he was apparently a committed Nazi and only managed to secure his release with the help of influential friends before going on to play an important role in organising the underground movement of Austrian Nazis. He was eventually once more taken into custody but again managed to flee and reached Germany where he advised the Berlin Security Police on Austrian-Italian political affairs. He was next sent to work in Abyssinia where he acted as a personal bodyguard to Emperor Haile Selassie whilst also spying on him for German intelligence. At the outbreak of the war he was a senior police official in Salzburg and, according to the account he gave to the British journalist twenty years later, in 1939 he was called up and joined the *Sicherheitsdienst*, the security arm of the *Schutzstaffeln* or 'SS', and served throughout the war. A US post-war interrogation indicated that in mid-December 1939 he had transferred from an initial fairly menial posting to join the *Geheime Feldpolizei* and a unit, 611, based in the Hanover military district. This unit received its orders at this stage of the war from German military intelligence, the *Abwehr*, and most of its recruits were former police officers.[11]

Once again the official and unofficial records diverge. It is known that Begus was appointed captain and also acted as an instructor until the attack on the Low Countries at which point he claimed to have then been selected to lead the specially selected group who attempted to capture Queen Wilhelmina, the attack which so alarmed the British authorities and most likely led to the establishment of the Coats Mission. Whilst some troops parachuted over the official royal residence at The Hague, his unit was amongst those involved in air-landing operations that in many cases resulted in transport aircraft crashing at the nearby Valkenburg airport.[12] From here his men had allegedly been tasked with rushing the Queen's palace whilst other German troops distracted Dutch ground forces. His target escaped and despite the heavy casualties suffered during this failed operation most of his unit were quickly recovered as the main advance of the

10 Thomas W. Lamb (Special Agent), 'Interrogation of BEGUS, Otto Dr.', Counter Intelligence Corps (Zell am See), 24 February 1950, Security Classified Intelligence and Investigative Dossiers (National Archives and Records Administration, Maryland), RG319, Box 671

11 Ibid., Wilhelm Krichbaum, 'The Secret Field Police', Historical Division European Command, 18 May 1947, MS# C-029; 'Geheime Feld Polizei', WO204/12996, TNA; ibid., 'Krichbaum Wilhelm', WO208/4356. According to the records at Yad Vashem the unit was also tasked with "the suppression of all forms of resistance in the occupied territories" and as the war developed so did its involvement in the atrocities conducted across Occupied Europe; 'Secret Field Police Group 611', Yad Vashem, http://db.yadvashem.org/deportation/agencyDetails.html?language=en &itemId=11091222

12 Amersfoort and Kamphuis (eds.), *May 1940: The Battle for the Netherlands*, pp.179-203. This is one of the most glaring errors in the Begus account as he talks about the target being the "official residence at Ruygenhoek". The Dutch Royal Family had moved to Noordeinde Palace where a secure bunker had been built for them and captured German maps showed this as a target for the airborne forces; 'The Royal Family – War Over Holland', http://www.waroverholland.nl/index. php?page=the-royal-family]

German military moved forward into the Netherlands. According to his records, Begus was next in Rotterdam and Amsterdam before moving into northern France and eventually on to Paris where he was promoted to Commissioner in charge of security of XVIII Army Corps. In this role he conducted counter espionage and troop security work across northern France until January 1941 before serving in similar roles in the Balkans and Greece. His final wartime role was in Verona, Italy where he was responsible for helping recruit and train saboteurs who were to be used against the then advancing Allied troops.

According to his post-war interviews he claimed that he actually returned to Germany directly following the end of the French campaign and it was from here that he received written instructions four weeks later in August 1940 to report for a special mission.[13] Within three days of receiving his initial orders he had arrived at a specially selected villa in Boulogne previously owned by a wealthy French industrialist, which would be used to plan the British mission. Direction and approval for planning was provided via a special scrambled phone which allowed for calls from the *Abwehr* headquarters in Munster and meant that there was no need for any written orders. This perhaps accounts for why no reference has ever been found to the mission in the surviving official German records nor is there any mention in accounts discussing the wartime role of German special military units.[14] According to Begus it was Hitler himself who devised the scheme believing that were it to succeed Britain would be forced to surrender. The German leader, who had also personally overseen the planning for the attempted capture of Queen Wilhelmina and did not view this mission as having been a complete failure, believed that "if those heads of state who were much loved by their people could be captured, they could be used as a surety for the good behaviour of the population".[15] For his new proposed operation, during a telephone briefing in a special security protected room an unnamed official confirmed the aims and the 41 year old Begus was given the authority to select his men and begin the planning. The mission was to be organised around a *Kommando* unit consisting of himself and 23 other SS officers, the rump of which had accompanied him on the Holland mission and the remainder selected for their fitness and courage and parachute training. He was provided with detailed plans of the Palace and the surrounding area along with the previously known defences, and briefings were given using photographs of the King and Queen along with other members of the Royal Family in conditions of great secrecy.

13 Clarke, *England Under Hitler*, pp.23-39
14 Leo Kessler, *Kommando – Hitler's Special Forces in the Second World War* (London; Leo Cooper, 1995); James Lucas, *Kommando – German Special Forces of World War Two* (London; Arms and Armour Press, 1985); Franz Kurowski, *The Brandenburger Commandos* (Mechanicsburg, PA; Stackpole Books, 2005), p.68; Eric Lefevre, *Brandenburg Division – Commandos of the Reich* (Paris; Histoire and Collections, 2000), pp.99-105; Ian Westwell, *Brandenburgers – the Third Reich's Special Forces* (Hersham; Ian Allan Publishing, 2003), pp.21-24
15 Clarke, *England Under Hitler*, p.29

Aerial photograph of Buckingham Palace and surrounding area taken prior to the start of the Second World War. Although obstacles would have been placed to prevent gliders from landing there were still large spaces to the rear of the palace and in Green Park to the west and north-west. This was the photograph included in the German guide, *Militärgeographische Angaben über England, London*, the second edition of which was published on 1 September 1940, and was listed as photograph number 24 'Die Residenz'.

This led to the production of a draft plan in which there would be an initial intensive dive-bombing attack on the defences around the target before about 400 paratroopers landed in Hyde Park, Green Park and St James's Park their role being to neutralise defences and hold up any counter-attacks.[16] A further 100 paratroopers were to drop directly into the grounds of Buckingham Palace using low-flying aircraft which were to approach the target in close waves to ensure that they dropped in the shortest possible time. With this done the men of the special 'Royal Unit' were to rush the apartments and secure any members of the Royal Family that could be found; it was estimated that the entire mission could be completed in 10 minutes. Great emphasis was placed upon the hostages being captured alive and the commandos were told not to conduct physical searches and to treat their captives with respect and courtesy. They were to be assembled in one room and details were even provided of how they were to be addressed with it being explicitly ordered that they be saluted in a traditional fashion and not with the Nazi salute before being addressed as follows: "The German High

16 Ibid, p.34

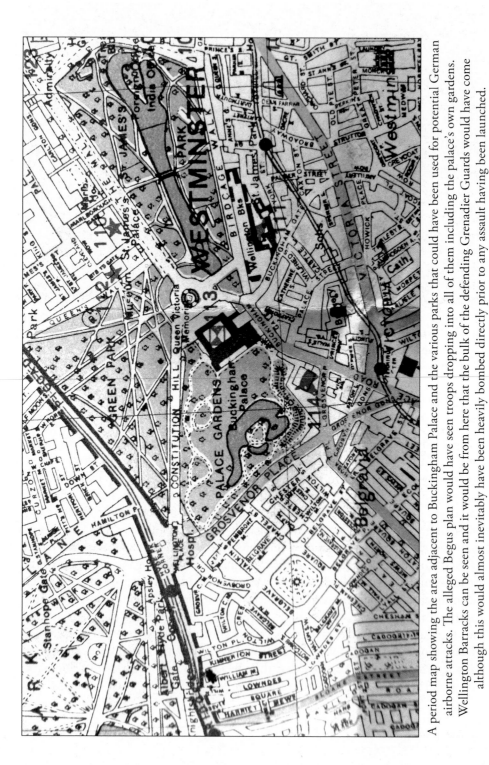

A period map showing the area adjacent to Buckingham Palace and the various parks that could have been used for potential German airborne attacks. The alleged Begus plan would have seen troops dropping into all of them including the palace's own gardens. Wellington Barracks can be seen and it would be from here that the bulk of the defending Grenadier Guards would have come although this would almost inevitably have been heavily bombed directly prior to any assault having been launched.

Command presents its respectful compliments. My duty, on the instructions of the Fuhrer, is to inform you that you are under the protection of the German Armed Forces".[17] Only with the failure to achieve air superiority during the Battle of Britain did enthusiasm for the plan begin to disappear and within three weeks of its formation the unit had been 'stood down' – presumably at some stage in mid-September 1940 – although it remained at the Boulogne headquarters until February of the following year.

The Germans were certainly at the forefront of using airborne forces to conduct critically important missions. During the attack against the Low Countries, aside from those paratroopers and glider-borne troops who were used in Holland, there were other highly innovative operations in Belgium. The first was the daring and decisive attack to seize the fortress at Eben Emael, and the other, Operation 'Niwi', an air-landing assault which captured key border fortifications and helped support the rapid advance of German armoured forces through the Ardennes to the French frontier.[18] The reality was, however, that Germany had never actually developed any prior formal plan for the invasion of Britain.[19] There had been some theoretical studies and a practical test with the occupation of the Channel Islands in June 1940, although the Germans realised that it would be unwise to compare the experiences gained from an attack on this lightly defended locality with the challenge of invading the mainland.[20] This meant that there was no consolidated plan, none of the required landing craft had been built, the already limited German navy had been further reduced during the campaigns fought up to that point, and the threat posed by the RAF remained a very real one. Hitler, like his planners, appeared to believe that the British would soon surrender. Only as it became clear that British resistance was not broken did the German leader's focus move with some greater measure of conviction towards a possible invasion, and this resulted on 2 July 1940 with the *Oberkommando der Wehrmacht* (OKW) confirming that the German leader had formally ordered that preparations be made. The outline plan called for six divisions to assault an area between Ramsgate and Bexhill, four more were to land between Brighton and the Isle of Wight and a final three would seek to create a bridgehead at Lyme Bay. The first wave would involve 90,000 troops assisted by airborne units with up to nine panzer and motorized divisions providing additional reinforcements. The first objective was to secure a line from Gravesend to Southampton, and the second between Maldon and the Severn, surrounding London. With the British capital

17 Ibid, pp.35-36
18 Jean-Michel Veranneman de Watervliet, *Belgium in the Second World War* (Barnsley; Pen and Sword, 2014), pp.1-4; Karl-Heinz Frieser (with John T. Greenwood), *The Blitzkrieg Legend: The 1940 Campaign in the West* (Annapolis, Maryland; Naval Institute Press, 2013), pp.122-127
19 Hans Umbrit, "Plans and Preparations for a Landing in England" in Klaus Maier et al., *Germany and the Second World War: Vol. 2, Germany's Initial Conquests in Europe* (Oxford; Clarendon Press, 1991), pp. 366-373.
20 Fleming, *Invasion 1940*, pp.264-267

occupied motorized divisions would then move north heading for Liverpool, Glasgow, Boston, Hull and Newcastle.

Despite there being no evidence of the 'Royal Unit' this lack of official documentation or material is not entirely surprising, such was the sensitive and highly secret nature of its mission. According to recently released post-war interrogations there was certainly planning for irregular operations as part of the main attack. Members of the elite German *Brandenburger* unit were to help give the appearance of the invasion taking place at several points along the English coast, in Scotland and in Southern Ireland.[21] At the same time, whilst the main attack would be centred on the Dover area shock troops wearing British uniforms were to conduct airborne landings directly prior to the arrival of the main attacking force. In light of what happened in Copenhagen, Oslo and The Hague, there was some written evidence to support Begus' claims that Hitler favoured targeting royalty. Indeed there was a German Armed Forces Supreme Command dated 2 April 1940 which stated that, "the Fuhrer has directed that the escape of the kings of Denmark and Norway from their countries at the time of occupation must be prevented by all means … It will be essential to keep the residences of the sovereigns under surveillance and, if necessary, to prevent the kings from leaving their palaces. … In that manner in which these measures are carried out, due regard will be given to the positions of the sovereigns as far as that is possible".[22] If King George VI, his wife or his daughters could be captured there was the potential to exploit the British people and terrorise them into submission. Should this aspect of the mission fail there was also, of course, the potential for a replacement monarch to put on the throne.

The potential role to be played by the King's brother, the Duke of Windsor, remains a controversial one and has done since 1954 when it was first revealed that Hitler's agents had monitored him closely and made approaches about his taking over in the event of a German victory.[23] As one writer has put it, when he was contacted in the summer of 1940 he gave the ambiguous response that he thought the most important thing was to end the war as quickly as possible.[24] Combined with his lingering animosity about his abdication and the poor treatment he felt he and his wife had received, along with his previously professed admiration for Germany, this has allowed various commentators to suggest that he could have considered doing something dramatic. At the war's outbreak the Duke had been living in effective exile in Paris and volunteered his assistance, eventually being

21 "Interrogation of Johannes Carl", 6 March 1945, KV2/3300, TNA
22 'Documents on German Foreign Policy, 1918-1945, Series D, Vol. IX', cited in Fleming, *Invasion 1940*, p.143
23 Andrew Morton, *17 Carnations: The Windsors, The Nazis and the Cover-up* (London; Michael O'Mara Books Limited, 2015), pp.172-195; Cadbury, *Princes at War*, pp.145, 153-154, 161-164, 171-188
24 Lacey, *Majesty*, p.139; Rachael Bletchley, 'Queen and Queen Mother kept British hope alive in World War Two and Hitler hated them', *Daily Mirror*, 18 July 2015

attached in October 1939 in a liaison role to the British Expeditionary Force. With the defeat of France he and his wife the Duchess of Windsor had moved south through the country traveling on to Spain and then in to Portugal where they eventually arrived in Lisbon.[25] Despite some considerable reluctance within the Royal Family it was agreed that the best course of action was that proposed by Churchill, to send the Duke to be the governor of the Bahamas, and he was asked to leave mainland Europe as quickly as possible.

Edward initially refused and sent away the first two flying boats that arrived to carry him and his wife back to Britain. At the same time he held a meeting with emissaries sent by the German Foreign Minister Joachim von Ribbentrop, who had previously been the ambassador in London and knew that the former King viewed the war as being an unnecessary one. The Duke was only eventually persuaded to leave after a fortnight spent in Lisbon intriguing and he finally departed on the first day of August 1940; he kept in touch with his German contacts for at least another year and is alleged to have indicated to them that if the word came he would return to Britain immediately.[26] The most detailed account of these events has concluded, "In the calm atmosphere of today no one would attribute actual guilt in the sense of deliberate treachery to the Duke, but comparative guilt is easier to estimate, and there is no doubt that his actions would have earned serious reprisals in the atmosphere of, for instance, the French Resistance".[27] There is no way of knowing how a puppet King would have been responded to by his subjects nor is there any real way of assessing the accuracy of the captured German intelligence documents which purport to tell the story. As the governess Marion Crawford later put it, what did happen was that for the remainder of the war "[Edward's] name was never mentioned" either at the Palace or at Windsor.[28] It is not known if any reference was ever made to Begus and his alleged 'Royal Unit'.

25 Roberts, *Eminent Churchillians*, pp.45-48
26 Shawcross, *Queen Elizabeth*, pp.518-521; Lacey, *Majesty*, p.140
27 Frances Donaldson, *Edward VIII* (London; Weidenfeld and Nicolson, 1974), p.377
28 Crawford, *The Little Princesses*, p.86

8

Another Mission

There is an interesting postscript to the story of the Coats Mission with a good deal of evidence indicating that an updated version existed during the Cold War with the same role, safeguarding the Royal Family's security but now in the event of a nuclear conflict. Prior to the Cuban Missile Crisis there had been some considera-tion of the subject but this was termed as a requirement for "special guard duties during a period of rising international tension" and involved less than 30 men.[1] In October 1963 the War Office had given some direction about what the 'Special Duties Force' should do as part of 'Operation Candid'; although no detailed tasks were designated the force would be responsible for guarding and escorting the Queen and other members of the Royal Family.[2] The matter was discussed in some detail over the months that followed and by April 1965 it was reiterated that this body, which was sometimes also referred to as 'Royal Duties Force', was to be given top priority in general war planning. There was also confirmation that in the event of an emergency, and once the government moved from London, the Queen "would probably move to an undisclosed place of residence, either by rail, road or air, and other members of the Royal Family would move to other desti-nations"; as had been the case with the 'Rocking Horse' plan, consideration was clearly being given to the Heir apparent. If the Royal Family travelled by rail or air the bulk of its bodyguard were to travel independently by road and join them at their refuges.[3]

The bodyguard looked very similar to its predecessor in terms of the basic structure with the fighting force being the Guards battalion then stationed at Windsor supported by an air-portable armoured reconnaissance squadron from the Household Cavalry, in addition to which there was dedicated signals troops and a REME Light Aid Detachment. It was, however, much larger as was apparent from the transport section which at its maximum proposed levels, later revised downwards, contained 32 vehicles some of which had trailers carrying stores and water along with two ambulances. Mobilised by HQ Eastern Command based in

---

1 The detachment consisted of 1 officer, 3 NCOs and 24 other ranks; 'Subject Guards', 6 February 1962, WO32/21796, TNA
2 Ibid., 'Operation Instruction – The Protection of the Royal Family in an Emergency (Plan Candid)', 13 July 1964; 'Protection of the Royal Family in an Emergency', 13 July 1964
3 Ibid., 'Reasons for the Proposal', 2 April 1964; 'Equipment For a Force for Special Duties (Operation Candid)', Equipment Quantities Committee – Meeting to be Held on Wednesday 7th April 1965; Lieutenant Colonel W.G.H. Beach, 'Protection of the Royal Family in War, 19 March 1965; in the large file of correspondence there is one reference to the 'Op CANDID Force'

Hounslow in Middlesex, which would instruct the component commanders to open sealed instructions on receipt of the 'Candid' code-word, this independent force was held at seven days readiness and would initially concentrate at Windsor with the intention being for it to be able to produce at least two of its designated rifle companies within a day of the alert being sounded. Once assembled, and operating under the overall command of the commanding officer of the Guards battalion, it would then be able to operate in a self-contained mobile manner for a period of seven days.[4] It was also to be prepared to split into four self-contained sub-unit groups which could move to different locations the secrecy of which was such that they had not been disclosed even to the Ministry of Defence.[5]

Some suggestion has been made that one of these sites, the only one to be referred to in the available planning documents where it is termed 'Key point 17', was a specially prepared underground suite of rooms for the Royal Family at the Central Government War Headquarters at Spring Quarry near Corsham in Wiltshire. This site, officially referred to as 'Site 3 Corsham', was known by various names including 'Turnstile' and 'Burlington' and had been prepared between 1954 and 1961 at great expense. It was designed to hold up to 6000 people living in frugal conditions who had the role of attempting to govern the country following a nuclear war. The rooms in 'Area 17 south' were completed to a much better standard and included two of the only three baths available across the entire complex.[6] Divisional headquarters or districts at which the 'Royal Duties Force' might arrive once war had broken out were to be given instructions in a sealed envelope explaining their role which was only to be opened once the code word 'Candid' was received.[7] As they travelled the country the force would be reliant on these headquarters to allow them to communicate for additional orders with GHQ Land Forces who would in turn receive guidance from what remained of the government; the commanding officer of the small force would also be able to receive instruction from the Royal Household.[8] In order to facilitate its movement the commander was to have been made aware of arrangements

4   Ibid., 'Plan Candid – Background', 23 March 1965; 'Protection of the Royal Family (Plan CANDID)', 15 May 1965; Lieutenant General K.T. Darling (GOC-in-C Eastern Command), 'Operation Instruction No.24 – Special Duties Force in General War', March 1965
5   Ibid., 'Equipment for a Force for Special Duties', Beach, 4 August 1965. Later Lieutenant General Sir Hugh Beach, who served as Commandant of the Staff College and was Deputy Commander of UK Land Forces
6   Ibid., 'Reasons for the Proposal', 2 April 1964; Steve Fox, 'Top Secret Acid – The Story of the Central Government War Headquarters', *Subterranea* (April 2010; Issue 22), pp.55-56; Justin Pollard, 'Burlington – the underground city that never was', *Engineering and Technology Magazine*, 15 August 2011
7   'Protection of the Royal Family in an Emergency', 13 July 1964, WO32/21796, TNA; ibid., 'Communications for Special Duties Force', Lieutenant Colonel R.J.G. Heaven, 17 May 1965
8   Ibid., 'Operation Instruction – The Protection of the Royal Family in an Emergency (Plan Candid)', 13 July 1964

made with the Royal Navy and the Royal Air Force which could impact upon him.[9]

An October 1968 report referred to an entire infantry battalion, approximately 400 men, still being assigned for 'special duties' towards the Royal Family with an equivalent number also earmarked for a similar role with Central Government and another battalion providing security for the country's gold reserves and art treasures.[10] According to a note written in June 1972 by Brigadier Ted Eberhardie, the B.G.S. Ops at the Land Forces Headquarters, 'Candid' had been cancelled "three years" before and he was keen to establish if it had been replaced by a new plan as considerable quantities of stores and vehicles were still being held at Ludgershall.[11] Reports in May and August 1973 noted that 'Candid' had been replaced with a new code word and the details revised.[12] Whilst it is not clear from the available information if this was the replacement, Plan 'Synchronise' had already been approved by the Cabinet Office when it was sent in December 1968 to GHQ UK Land Forces and HQ London District as a draft document for comment.[13] It was described as replacing the 'Candid' operation instruction and was intended to be put into effect during the period immediately prior to General Mobilisation. Much as had been the case prior to the outbreak of the Second World War, it assumed that the Queen and other members of the Royal Family would move to "their wartime place of residence" when the government moved from London and what was now referred to as the 'Special Duties battalion', would provide guards. This force had been reduced in size earlier that year and was now intended to normally be drawn from the Public Duties battalion already at Windsor. The plan called for the Royal Family to be moved from London by air with the battalion, less any immediate escorts and the commanding officer, still travelling by road to meet up with them; speculation persists that the Broad Walk in Kensington Gardens was adapted in the 1950s to land an aircraft for such a purpose but helicopters would have been much better suited for the role.[14]

Despite the changes the requirement was retained that the battalion would still be split into four groups each of which was to be capable of moving independently by road to any part of the country. The first of these, known as 'Party VICTOR', was an advance party which was to prepare a barracks to be used by the remainder of the battalion 'Party X-RAY'. 'Party YANKEE' was a separate platoon which

9   Ibid., Lieutenant Colonel Rob Heaven, 'Protection of the Royal Family', 6 July 1964
10 'Military Aspects of the Home Defence of the United Kingdom', 1 October 1968, DEFE 4/232, TNA
11 Brigadier C.E. Eberhardie to Brigadier P. Hudson, 8 June 1972, WO32/21796, TNA; correspondence elsewhere in the file suggests that it was cancelled in May 1969
12 Ibid., Major B.J. Beattie, 'Plan Candid', 14 May 1973; Major A.E. Cornick, 'Earmark of Equipment/Stores', 6 August 1973
13 Ibid., Major General C.H. Blacker (Director of Army Staff Duties), 'The Protection of the Royal Family in an Emergency', 11 December 1968
14 Elizabeth Day, 'Secret files reveal plans to evacuate the Queen before a Soviet nuclear attack', *Daily Telegraph*, 28 March 2004

was to undertake an undisclosed mission whilst 'Party ZULU' acted as the rear party and would move immediately the Queen had left London. On receipt of the code-word 'Clasp', which indicated the beginning of a period of tension, the commanding officer was to report to the Director of Army Staff Duties who would give him his orders and, presumably, the different parties would begin undertaking their previously assigned tasks.

According to one of the few published accounts to have examined the War Book preparations for the Cold War period, from 1954 onwards, with the royal yacht, HMY Britannia, having been commissioned, the decision was taken that this would be used to carry Queen Elizabeth II to a place of safety.[15] Even with this author's privileged access to sources and information, he was not able to discover the contingency in the event of a surprise attack but he speculated that it involved "a safe place somewhere on terra firma (almost certainly in Scotland)". Balmoral was unlikely to have been used as it was a known location but there were no shortage of other large houses scattered around the Highlands. An updated version of this study, published in 2010 and drawing upon newly released documents, provided further details about what was termed the 'Python' system which proposed to disperse the machinery of government in time of war.[16] This proposed approach the 'Black Move' of its day, had been introduced in May 1968 and was intended to involve the movement of 1200 people away from London to alternate locations.[17] The original claims were developed further to propose that Queen Elizabeth and the Duke of Edinburgh would have been moved around the sea lochs of north-west Scotland with HMY Britannia acting as a 'floating bunker'. When the plans for the vessel's construction were approved in 1952 it was also proposed that up to 200 patients could be accommodated during a conflict and this official role continued for forty years.[18] Investigations by independent historians would appear to have established that in addition to its designated secondary purpose of acting as a hospital ship, there was also a home defence role.[19]

As would be expected, no information exists about the current position and what additional security has been provided for the Royal Family in the event of a national emergency which might require they be moved away from Greater London. It must, however, be assumed that measures have been taken and it is to be hoped that there remains a modern equivalent of the Coats Mission.

15 Peter Hennessy, *The Secret State: Whitehall and the Cold War* (London; Allen Lane, The Penguin Press, 2002), p.176
16 Simon Johnson, '"Floating bunker" plan to help Queen escape nuclear attack', *Daily Telegraph*, 12 July 2010. Lord Hennessy repeated the claims as recently as October 2014 although he confirmed that he had not seen any detailed plans; Sanchia Berg, 'The nuclear attack on the UK that never happened', *BBC News*, 30 October 2014
17 'Machinery of Government in War', 6 November 1967, MAF250/315, TNA
18 *The Royal Yacht Britannia – Official Souvenir Guidebook* (Edinburgh; Someone Publishing Ltd., 2013), pp.39, 58
19 'Linstock', 'FT Cockchafer and the 1975 Dorset BW Detection Trials', (Blog) 4 March 2010, http://www.shipsnostalgia.com/showpost.php?p=406913&postcount=15

Conclusions

Reading his account and some of the detailed intelligence files which examined his post-war career as a triple agent working for the various Cold War protagonists, Begus does have the appearance of an opportunist and, perhaps even, a fantasist. There are also doubts and questions with only limited writtten material available to test the claims he made. Yet there is evidence confirming the value Hitler attached to small airborne operations with high value targets. Later in the war Otto Skorzeny led groups of *Kommandos* in operations the aim of which was to seize key figures who the German leader believed had a potentially critical value; the deposed Italian leader Benito Mussolini was perhaps the most famous but there were a number of other missions.[1] There was also the April 1940 German Armed Forces Supreme Command which had specifically targeted European sovereigns and the value which was to be attached to them. Whilst the activities of Coats and his men was known only to a very few there was a real concern amongst Britain's senior military and political leaders about the potential danger posed by enemy airborne forces and this definitely extended to the security of the Royal Family. This could be seen with decisions such as that taken in October 1940 to increase from two to ten the number of Bren carriers available to the defenders of Windsor Castle "to deal with possible enemy parachutists" but there were others that were made.[2] Perhaps more significantly the following summer, in July 1941, General Alan Brooke, now the Chief of the Imperial General Staff, expressed his concern about the potential threat of parachute landings in London highlighting the danger presented by the city's large parks which could be used by German airborne troops.[3] Despite his efforts to organise a major exercise that would test the defences his proposal was eventually rejected due to concerns about what effect this would have undermining public morale.

While it never had to test its readiness in an actual emergency, the one trial that took place in potentially similar conditions, only weeks after it had been established, seemed to suggest that the Coats Mission was prepared to carry out its role. With conditions felt to be ideal for an invasion attempt, when the 'Cromwell' alert was issued on 7 September 1940 to indicate an attack was believed imminent, the Coldstreamers packed and made ready to move. Once the alert had passed, they "returned to a familiar routine of rehearsing the role

---

1   Charles Foley, *Commando Extraordinary: The Spectacular Exploits of Otto Skorzeny* (London; Pan, 1956); Charles Whiting, *Skorzeny* (Barnsley; Pen and Sword, 2010)
2   Minute by Alan Brooke, 17 October 1940, WO199/287, TNA
3   Diary, 9 July 1941, cited in Danchev and Todman (eds.), *War Diaries 1939-1945*, pp.169-170; Arthur Bryant, *The Turn of the Tide* (London; Collins, 1957), p.242

of a mobile column – getting into buses, fighting from them, and getting out again".[4] That same evening, troops from the Morris Detachment were out on one of their practice runs when they were stopped by a Home Guard road block. On learning of the potential threat they turned round and drove back to Windsor also ready to carry out the role for which they had been rehearsing.[5] On their return they found some initial confusion amongst the garrison when it was discovered that the Grenadier Guards Duty Officer did not know what the code-word meant and his code-book was locked in the safe. He was therefore forced to travel from Victoria Barracks to Combermere Barracks to ask his colleagues in the Household Cavalry if they knew what was happening.[6] The Duty Squadron eventually turned out and headed to the nearby Langley airfield and the only incident of note was that "a Troop Leader ... an officer of some seniority, who had seen service in the First World War, after failing to get an answer to his challenge to some dim form that appeared in the darkness, fired his revolver and found that he had shot a cart horse".[7] This provided clear evidence that not everybody was as well prepared, even at this stage early in their training, as the officers and men in the Coats Mission and Morris Detachment.

In reality it is impossible to say what might have happened or even the exact details of the plans that were prepared to protect the King and Queen and their two daughters in the event of a German attack which aimed to kill or capture them. It had apparently been agreed at the outset that when material designated 'GHQ Operation Instruction, Special No.A' was updated the old documents were to be destroyed by fire with a destruction certificate sent back to the Home Forces headquarters and, in April 1943, an envelope of instructions marked 'Most Secret – Coats Mission (Papers)' was destroyed.[8] The removal of any associated documentation even extended to a group photograph which was taken at an early point in the Mission's existence but nobody saw it and it must presumably have been destroyed with the other papers.[9] The process was also extremely thorough and with the Mission's formal conclusion, at the end of December 1944 any remaining documents were destroyed by fire including an envelope of old papers and maps showing essential traffic routes that were to have been followed.[10] This helps explain why when Clarke, who was preparing to interview Begus at his

---

4   Howard and Sparrow, *The Coldstream Guards*, p.21
5   'Memories of the Coats Mission', Darell Papers
6   Orde, *Second Household Cavalry Regiment*, p.5
7   Ibid.
8   Minute, 3 April 1943, WO199/292, TNA
9   Darell to author, 29 June 2010. His investigations also revealed that an unofficial diary kept by Tatham and handed over to Tubb when had had taken command, had been "mislaid" at some subsequent stage. There was also no response to an appeal about whether Jimmy Coats had ever kept any papers; Darell to Andy (?), 8 September 1988, 'Sir Jeffrey Lionel Darell Bt., MC, P/95569', CGRA
10 Minute, 29 December 1944, WO199/298, TNA. These had been gathered together back in December 1942 when the decision had been first taken that the mission should be stood down

home in Austria, telephoned back to London to enquire if anything was known about an attempt to kidnap the King, as he put it, "eventually the answer came – nothing at all".[11] There has continued to be a lack of willingness to discuss the wartime preparations. In 1985 a BBC documentary examining the Queen Mother's experience of the Second World War had proposed initially to include some reference to the Coats Mission. The Coldstream regimental headquarters had confirmed with Darell that he was willing to be interviewed and arrangements had been made for Ludovic Kennedy to meet with him before the Chief of the General Staff's office intervened and insisted that the subject not be raised on the grounds of it still being classified.[12]

In the absence of definitive information and a continuing lack of official support, there will inevitably remain speculation about the possible plans and outcomes. According to his official biographer it was apparently the King's intention that "in the event of a German occupation of the country, [he would] ... offer his immediate services, in any capacity, to the leader of a British resistance movement".[13] Another historian, however, has concluded that it was doubtful whether the King would have been allowed to stay in the event of invasion, writing that he would have been eventually evacuated to Canada in a common-sense move via "one of the four large country houses earmarked as refuges".[14] As this assessment features in an often critical account of Churchill's actions during the summer of 1940, part of an attack on him for misleading the House of Commons on what the King would do, its value has been questioned.[15] Nonetheless this is a commonly argued view, the King would have had to agree in the end to the Royal Family being evacuated, whether to Canada or elsewhere. He had been critical of the decision by King Leopold not to leave Belgium and set up a government-in-exile and it is difficult to see how he would have allowed himself to become a hostage or some form of puppet king.[16] The Canadian leader William Mackenzie King had written in his often controversial diary at the end of May 1940 that the King and Queen could soon be arriving, the inference being that they would have to leave a defeated Britain and there were rumours in London at the time that this was about to happen.[17]

11 Clarke, *England Under Hitler*, p.27
12 Major D.N. Thornewill (Regimental Adjutant, Coldstream Guards), 'File – Brig Darell: Coats Mission', 9/11 July 1985', 'Sir Jeffrey Lionel Darell Bt., MC, P/95569', CGRA
13 Wheeler-Bennett, *King George VI*, p.463; Aronson, *The Royal Family at War*, p.29
14 Roberts, *Eminent Churchillians*, pp.42-43
15 Anthony Howard, 'Heroes and villains' (Review), *The Sunday Times*, 24 July 1994; Vernon Bogdanor, 'From bulldog spirit to lapdog ways' (Review), *The Times Higher Education*, March 3, 1995. The latter, highly respected reviewer went so far as to condemn Robert's work as having "little value as a work of history"
16 Aronson, *The Royal Family at War*, p.30
17 Diary, 27 May 1940, 'Diaries of William Lyon Mackenzie King' (Libraries and Archives Canada, Ottawa), http://www.bac-lac.gc.ca/eng/discover/politics-government/prime-ministers/william-lyon-mackenzie-king/Pages/diaries-william-lyon-mackenzie-king.aspx

It is perhaps best to draw as much as possible upon the limited information that has been provided by the key figures to reach any conclusions. When Churchill had been shown a proposal in late May 1940 that he, the government and the Royal Family should be evacuated in the event of an invasion he replied that "no such discussion" was to be permitted.[18] Reflecting the weakness of his political position, this idea obviously continued to be discussed in some circles. The King himself was described by one source as having refused a Ministerial suggestion put to him at around the same time that the Princesses should be sent to Canada; when he had asked Churchill in mid-June 1940 if the two young girls would be a liability in the event of an invasion he had been assured that this would not be the case.[19] His wife was equally resolute in her decision. According to one account the Queen described the possibility of leaving Britain in simple terms, saying that "it just never occurred to us, we never gave it a thought".[20] More famously she was quoted as also saying that, "the children could not go without me [to Canada], I could not possibly leave the King, and the King would never go".[21] At the same time the Princesses' governess claimed that neither she nor Queen Elizabeth believed there would be an invasion, "it was a case of woman's intuition, but once again it was proved right".[22] Private comments made by the Queen many years later suggest that she may have felt differently writing to the Coldstreamers that "a German invasion was very much on the cards for the first year or so of the war".[23] And, according to the Queen Mother's recent biographer, the renewed invasion threat in the spring of 1941 resulted in discussions between the King and Churchill about the security of the Royal Family and the government. During these the Prime Minister reportedly reaffirmed that he planned to stay in London as long as possible and, according to this account, "the King knew that he would have to remain with the government – he could not delegate his powers. But the Queen and the Princesses would be rushed to the country".[24] Corbitt, who had been so intimately involved in making preparations for the possible move to one of the country residences, believed that King George VI never planned to leave London unless it was with the government and in the knowledge that his wife and children "had been evacuated to comparative safety".[25] Darell also was "absolutely convinced" that the King and Queen would never have left the country although "the Princesses might have been sent to Canada".[26] One of the few men who almost certainly knew what would happen was Jimmy Coats and whilst, in

18 'Monday 27 May 1940', in Addison and Crang (eds.), *Listening to Britain*, p.44; Martin Gilbert, *Churchill: A Life* (London; Pimlico, 2000), p.654

19 Bradford, *The Reluctant King*, p.321; Shawcross, *Queen Elizabeth*, p.517

20 Conversation with author, cited in Aronson, *The Royal Family at War*, p.28

21 Longford, *Queen Mother*, p.80

22 Crawford, *The Little Princesses*, p.117

23 Queen Elizabeth, The Queen Mother to Darell, n.d., Darell Papers

24 Shawcross, *Queen Elizabeth*, p.533

25 Corbitt, *My Twenty Years in Buckingham Palace*, p.161

26 Interview with Darell, 18 August 2010

the 1950s, he indicated he was willing to discuss the subject with Peter Fleming, there is no evidence that this took place and there was only a very brief reference to his Mission in the published volume.[27]

What is known is that the Coats Mission, a group of men predominantly drawn from the Coldstream Guards and the 12th Lancers, spent nearly two years working alongside one another preparing for a dreadful possibility. With Britain under attack and German forces attempting to invade they had been given the role to protect the Royal Family the security of which, certainly in 1940, was vital to the survival of the state. German airborne forces had made audacious attempts to seize European royalty but, for one of the officers, when asked about how it felt to be a member of a force "whose declared aim was to fight to the last round and the last man", this was "a marvellous honour" and there is no doubt this body-guard would have done its utmost to do its duty.[28] On learning that there had been a possible plan to attack Buckingham Palace, Darell very much hoped "we would have been in one of the houses by then".[29] Hopefully this would have been the case and the troops were at Madresfield Court with all of the Royal Family having been safely brought there by the Morris Detachment to join them. Dug in to mount their final defence, preparations would then perhaps have begun to carry out the 'Rocking Horse' plan in whatever form it existed and depending on the circumstances that faced the men who had been given this vitally important role. As it was this 'worst case scenario' was never tested, the heroic defence conducted by the Royal Air Force and the insatiable but ultimately disastrous lure that the Soviet Union presented to Adolf Hitler combined to leave the activities of the King's Private Army as a largely unknown but fascinating wartime anecdote.

27 Note by Peter Fleming, 27 September 1955, Fleming Papers, MS1391, A7, UoR
28 Interview with Hancock, 1984, IWM
29 Darell to author, 11 September 2010

Bibliography

Paul Addison and Jeremy A. Crang (eds.), *Listening to Britain: Home Intelligence Reports on Britain's Finest Hour – May to September 1940* (London; The Bodley Head, 2010)

Herman Amersfoort and Piet Kamphuis (eds.), *May 1940 – The Battle for the Netherlands* (Leiden; Brill, 2010)

Theo Aronson, *The Royal Family at War* (London; John Murray, 1994)

Bernard Ash, *Norway 1940* (London; Cassell, 1964)

David Birt, *The Battle of Bewdley* (Great Witley; Peter Huxtable Designs, 1988)

Brian Bond, *British Military Policy between the Two World Wars* (Oxford; Clarendon Press, 1980)

Russell Braddon, *All The Queen's Men – The Household Cavalry and the Brigade of Guards* (London; Hamish Hamilton, 1977)

Sarah Bradford, *The Reluctant King – The Life and Reign of George VI 1895-1952* (New York; St Martin's Press, 1990)

Lieutenant Colonel E.H. Brongers, *The Battle for the Hague 1940* (Soesterberg; Aspekt, 2004)

Arthur Bryant, *The Turn of the Tide* (London; Collins, 1957)

Paula Byrne, *Mad World – Evelyn Waugh and the Secrets of Brideshead* (London; Harper Press, 2009)

Deborah Cadbury, *Princes at War: The British Royal Family's Private Battle in the Second World War* (London; Bloomsbury, 2015)

Jeff Carpenter, *Wartime Worcestershire* (Studley; Brewin Books, 1995)

Comer Clarke, *England Under Hitler* (London; Consul Books, 1963)

Basil Collier, *The Defence of the United Kingdom (History of the Second World War)* (London; Her Majesty's Stationary Office, 1957)

F.J. Corbitt, *My Twenty Years in Buckingham Palace – A Book of Intimate Memoirs* (New York; David McKay Company Inc., 1956)

Marion Crawford, *The Little Princesses* (London; Orion, 2003)

Major S.F. Crozier, *The History of the Corps of Royal Military Police* (Aldershot; Gale and Polden Ltd., 1951)

Alex Danchev and Daniel Todman (eds.), *War Diaries, 1939-1945: Field Marshal Lord Alanbrooke* (London; Weidenfeld and Nicolson, 2001)

Charles De Gaulle, *The Call to Honour: 1940-1942* (London; Weidenfeld and Nicolson, 1955)

Douglas Dodds-Parker, *Setting Europe Ablaze – Some Account of Ungentlemanly Warfare* (London; Springwood Books, 1983)

Frances Donaldson, *Edward VIII* (London; Weidenfeld and Nicolson, 1974)

Richard Doherty, *Humber Light Reconnaissance Car 1941-45* (Oxford; Osprey Publishing, 2011)

David Erskine, *The Scots Guards, 1919-1955* (London; William Clowes and Sons Ltd., 1956)

Peter Fleming, *Invasion 1940* (London; Hart Davis, 1957)

Charles Foley, *Commando Extraordinary: The Spectacular Exploits of Otto Skorzeny* (London; Pan, 1956)

Karl-Heinz Frieser (with John T. Greenwood), *The Blitzkrieg Legend: The 1940 Campaign in the West* (Annapolis, Maryland; Naval Institute Press, 2013)

Martin Gilbert, *Churchill: A Life* (London; Pimlico, 2000)

Jack Greene and Alessandro Massignani, *Hitler Strikes North – The Nazi Invasion of Norway and Denmark, 9 April 1940* (London; Frontline Books, 2013)

Richard Greenway, *The Story of Madresfield Court* (Malvern; First Paige, 1991)

Brian Harwood, *Chivalry and Command: 500 Years of Horse Guards* (Oxford; Osprey Publishing, 2006)

Peter Hennessy, *The Secret State: Whitehall and the Cold War* (London; Allen Lane, The Penguin Press, 2002)

Richard Holmes, *Churchill's Bunker: The Secret Headquarters at the Heart of Britain's Victory* (London; Profile Books, 2011)

Michael Howard and John Sparrow, *The Coldstream Guards 1920-1946* (London; Oxford University Press, 1951)

Roy Jenkins, *Churchill* (London; Macmillan, 2001)

Denis Judd, *King George VI* (London; Michael Joseph, 1982)

Joseph P. Kennedy, *Hostage to Fortune – The Letters of Joseph P. Kennedy* (New York; Penguin, 2002)

François Kersaudy, *Norway 1940* (London; Arrow Books Limited, 1991)

Leo Kessler, *Kommando – Hitler's Special Forces in the Second World War* (London; Leo Cooper, 1995)

Halvdan Koht, *Norway – Neutral and Invaded* (London; Hutchinson and Co. Ltd., 1941)

Franz Kurowski, *The Brandenburger Commandos* (Mechanicsburg, PA; Stackpole Books, 2005)

Robert Lacey, *Majesty – Elizabeth II and the House of Windsor* (London; Hutchinson of London, 1977)

David Lampe, *The Last Ditch: Britain's Secret Resistance and the Nazi Invasion Plan* (London; Greenhill Books, 2007)

Eric Lefevre, *Brandenburg Division – Commandos of the Reich* (Paris; Histoire and Collections, 2000)

James Lucas, *Kommando – German Special Forces of World War Two* (London; Arms and Armour Press, 1985)

Henrik O. Lunde, *Hitler's Pre-Emptive War – The Battle for Norway, 1940* (Newbury; Casemate, 2011)

Walter B. Maas, *The Netherlands at War: 1940-1945* (London; Abelard-Schuman, 1970)

Klaus Maier et al., *Germany and the Second World War: Vol. 2, Germany's Initial Conquests in Europe* (Oxford; Clarendon Press, 1991)

Francis Mackay, *Overture to Overlord* (Barnsley; Pen and Sword, 2000)

Francis K. Mason, *Battle over Britain* (London; McWhirter Twins Ltd., 1969)

Leo McKinstry, *Operation Sealion: How Britain Crushed the German War Machine's Dream of Invasion in 1940* (London; John Murray, 2014)

Sir Owen Morshead, *Windsor Castle* (London; Phaidon Press Ltd., 1971)

Andrew Morton, *17 Carnations: The Windsors, The Nazis and the Cover-up* (London; Michael O'Mara Books Limited, 2015)

J.L. Moulton, *The Norwegian Campaign of 1940 – A Study of Warfare in Three Dimensions* (London; Eyre and Spottiswoode, 1966)

Hilda Newman (with Tim Tate), *Diamonds at Dinner: My Life as a Lady's Maid in a 1930s Stately Home* (London; John Blake Publishing Ltd., 2013)

Captain Nigel Nicolson and Patrick Forbes, *The Grenadier Guards in the War of 1939-1945 – Volume 1, The Campaigns in the North-West Europe* (Aldershot; Gale and Polden Limited, 1949)

Harold Nicolson (Nigel Nicolson, ed.), *Diaries and Letters: 1939-1945* (London; Collins, 1967)

Bernard O'Connor, *RAF Tempsford: Churchill's Most Secret Airfield* (Stroud; Amberley Publishing Limited, 2010)

Lynne Olson, *Citizens of London: The Americans Who Stood with Britain in its Darkest, Finest Hour* (New York; Random House, 2010)

Roden Orde, *The Household Cavalry at War: Second Household Cavalry Regiment* (Aldershot; Gale and Polden Ltd., 1953)

Mike Osborne, *20th Century Defences in Britain: The London Area* (Market Deeping; Concrete Publications, 2006)

Julian Paget, *The Story of the Guards* (London; Michael Joseph Ltd., 1979)

Julian Paget (ed.), *Second to None: The Coldstream Guards 1650-2000* (Yorkshire; Leo Cooper, 2000)

Jonathan Petropoulos, *Royals and the Reich: The Princes von Hessen in Nazi Germany* (Oxford; Oxford University Press, 2009)

Ben Pimlott, *The Queen – A Biography of Elizabeth II* (London; Harper Collins Publishers, 1997)

Margaret Rhodes, *The Final Curtsey – A Royal Memoir by the Queen's Cousin* (Edinburgh; Birlinn Limited, 2012)

Andrew Roberts, *Eminent Churchillians* (London; Weidenfeld and Nicolson, 1994)

William Sansom, *The Blitz: Westminster at War* (Oxford; Oxford University Press, 1990)

William Shawcross, *Queen Elizabeth the Queen Mother: The Official Biography* (London; Pan, 2010)

Clifford Smith, *The Great Park and Windsor Forest* (Windsor; Bank House Books, 2004)

Geoffrey Stewart, *Dunkirk and the Fall of France* (Barnsley; Pen and Sword, 2008)

Lord Strabolgi, *The Campaign in the Low Countries* (London; Hutchinson and Co. Ltd.; London, 1945)

Anthony Summers, *Conspiracy* (New York; McGraw-Hill, 1980)

John Terraine, *The Right of the Line: the Royal Air Force in the European War, 1939-1945* (London; Hodder and Stoughton, 1985)

Hugo Vickers, *Elizabeth – The Queen Mother* (London; Hutchinson, 2005)

Jean-Michel Veranneman de Watervliet, *Belgium in the Second World War* (Barnsley; Pen and Sword, 2014)

Ian Westwell, *Brandenburgers – the Third Reich's Special Forces* (Hersham; Ian Allan Publishing, 2003)

John W. Wheeler-Bennett, *King George VI – His Life and Reign* (London; Macmillan and Co. Ltd., 1958)

B.T. White, *Tanks and Other AFVs of the Blitzkrieg Era, 1939-1941* (London; Macmillan, 1972)

Charles Whiting, *Skorzeny* (Barnsley; Pen and Sword, 2010)

Mick Wilks, *The Defence of Worcestershire and the Southern Approaches to Birmingham in World War II* (Little Logaston; Logaston Press, 2007)

Mick Wilks, *Chronicles of the Worcestershire Home Guard* (Herefordshire; Logaston Press, 2014)

Colonel The Hon. Humphrey Wyndham M.C., *The Household Cavalry at War: First Cavalry Regiment* (Aldershot; Gale and Polden Ltd., 1952)

Philip Ziegler, *London at War 1939-1945* (London; Pimlico, 2002)

Index

INDEX OF PEOPLE

INDEX OF PLACES

INDEX OF MILITARY FORMATIONS & UNITS

INDEX OF MISCELLANEOUS TERMS